Grammar Rules!

Tanya Gibb

Australian Curriculum Edition

Name: ______________________________

Class: ______________________________

Grammar Rules! Student Book 5
Australian Curriculum Edition
ISBN: 978 0 6550 9253 7

Designer and typesetter: Trish Hayes
Illustrator: Stephen Michael King
Series editor: Marie James
Indigenous consultant: Al Fricker

Acknowledgement of Country
Matilda Education Australia acknowledges all Aboriginal and Torres Strait Islander Traditional Custodians of Country and recognises their continuing connection to land, sea, culture, and community. We pay our respects to Elders past and present.

This edition published in 2024 by **Matilda Education Australia**, an imprint of Meanwhile Education Pty
Melbourne, Australia
T: 1300 277 235
E: customersupport@matildaed.com.au
W: www.matildaeducation.com.au

First edition published in 2008 by Macmillan Science and Education Australia Pty Ltd

Publication data
Author: Tanya Gibb
Title: *Grammar Rules! Student Book 5 Australian Curriculum Edition*
ISBN: 978 0 6550 9253 7

A catalogue record for this book is available from the National Library of Australia

Printed in Australia by Pegasus Media & Logistics
January 2026

Contents

Note to Teachers and Parents

Grammar Rules!

Grammar Rules! comprehensively addresses the interrelated strands of Language, Literature and Literacy in the **Australian Curriculum English V9**, 2022. The *Grammar Rules!* series supports students' development of knowledge, understanding and skills in reading, viewing, speaking, writing and creating texts.

The **Australian Curriculum English** recognises that learning in English is recursive and cumulative, so each book in the *Grammar Rules!* series is designed to build on concepts covered previously and for an expanding range of audiences and purposes.

Grammar Rules! provides a conceptually sound scope and sequence of context-based activities that support teaching and learning in English. Although the title for the series is *Grammar Rules!*, the series in not just about grammar. Each unit of work in the series begins at the level of the whole text by identifying purpose and audience for the model text, providing teaching opportunities to activate students' background knowledge of the topic or the text type, and then supporting students in reading comprehension. The texts provided can be used for discussion of text forms and features and sentence structures, as well as for vocabulary expansion. The texts can also be used as models for students to use when creating their own written, spoken or multimodal texts. The texts included in *Grammar Rules!* cover a variety of informative, imaginative and persuasive texts and hybrid texts that use elements of different types of texts.

Grammar Rules! also teaches the conventions of punctuation and some aspects of spelling, such as prefixes, suffixes, apostrophes and homophones, and literary elements, such as onomatopoeia, simile and idiom, as well as character, setting and plot in narratives. *Grammar Rules!* comprehensively supports the aim of the **Australian Curriculum English V9** to 'help students learn to analyse, understand, communicate and build relationships with others and the world around them. It helps create confident communicators, imaginative and critical thinkers, and informed citizens.'

Student Book 5

Units of work

Student Book 5 contains 35 weekly units of work presented in a conceptually sound scope and sequence. The intention is for students to work through the units in the sequence in which they are presented. See the **Scope and Sequence Chart** on pages 6–7 for more information. The six Revision Units can be used for consolidation or assessment purposes.

The sample texts in *Student Book 5* are not tied to any particular content across other curriculum areas but are generally based on the theme of earth and space. This allows teachers and students to focus on the way language is structured in the different types of texts according to purpose and audience. Students can then use this knowledge to critically evaluate, respond to and create texts in other learning areas.

Icons

Encourages students to create texts of their own to demonstrate their understanding of the text structures and features taught in the unit. These activities focus on written language; however, many also provide opportunities for using spoken language to engage with others, make presentations and develop skills in using ICT.

Highlights useful grammatical rules and concepts. The rule is always introduced the first time students need it to complete an activity.

Tells students that a special hint is provided for an activity. It might be a tip about language features or a reminder to look at a rule in a previous unit.

Grammar Rules! Glossary

A valuable glossary is provided at the end of *Student Book 5*. Teachers and students can use this as a reference for terminology and rules introduced in *Student Book 5*. Page references are also given for the point in the book where the rule or tip was first introduced, so that students can go back to that unit if they need more information or further revision of the concept.

Pull-Out Writing Log

At the centre of *Student Book 5* is a practical pull-out Writing Log so that students can keep track of the texts they have created or attempted to create. The Writing Log also includes a handy reminder of the writing process, as well as a checklist of types of texts for students to try.

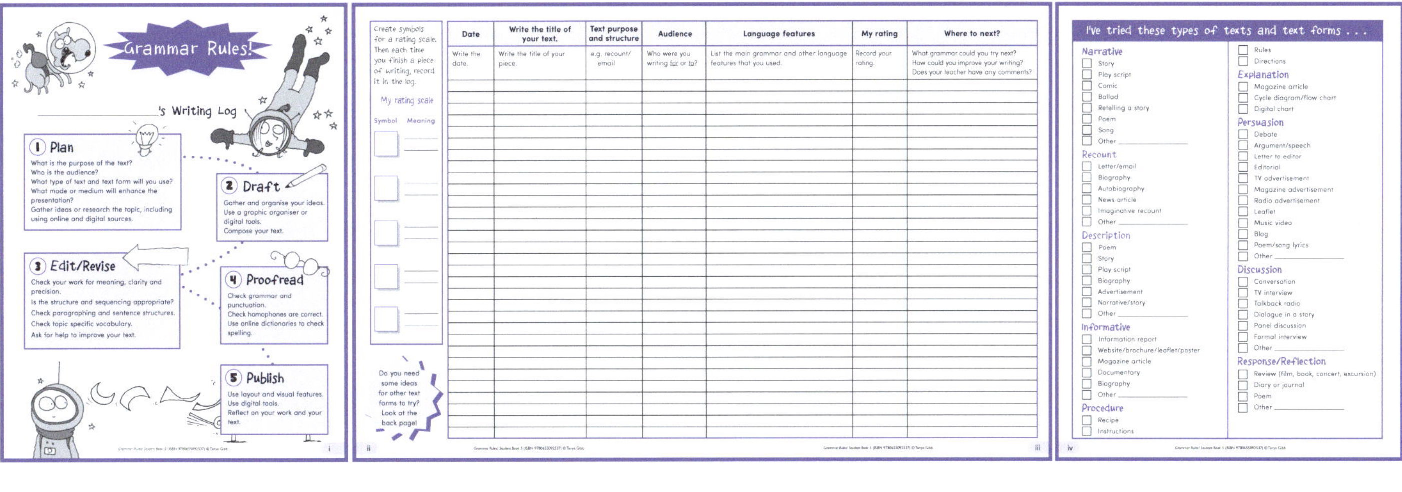

Unit At A Glance

Unit tag
States the main language focus

Type of text
Highlights the type of text and purpose of the sample text

Rule!
Introduces students to a new concept

Text sample
Provides a context for learning about language

Sequenced activities
Activities focus on reading comprehension, text features and structures, vocabulary, grammar or punctuation

Tip!
Reminds or gives a special hint

Try it yourself!
Gives students opportunities to apply their knowledge and skills to create their own texts. Students can engage in planning, drafting and editing their texts and using different modes and media to enhance presentation of their texts.

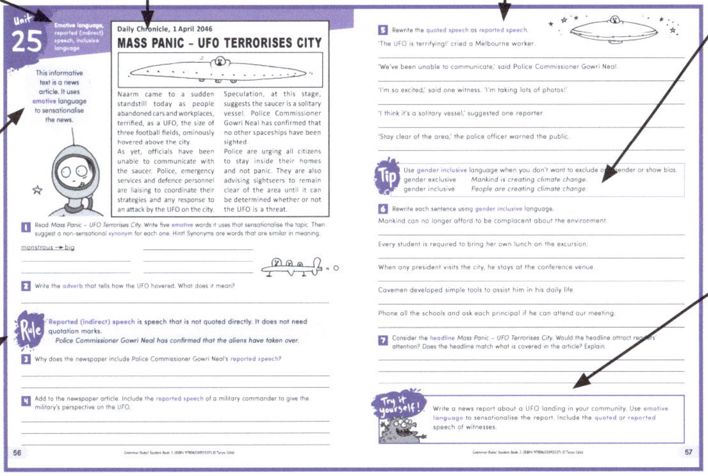

Grammar Rules! Teacher Resource Book 3–6

Full teacher support for *Student Book 5* is provided by *Grammar Rules! Teacher Resource Book 3–6*.

Here you will find valuable background information about teaching English along with practical resources, such as:

- strategies for teaching text structures and features
- literacy games and activities
- assessment strategies
- grammar and punctuation wall charts
- teaching tips for every unit in *Student Book 5*
- answers for every unit in *Student Book 5*.

Scope and Sequence

This scope and sequence chart is based on the requirements of the Australian Curriculum English.

Unit	Unit name Type of text	Purpose of text	Clauses, sentences, conjunctions, connectives	Nouns, noun groups, pronouns, adjectives	Verbs and verb groups	Adverbs, adverbials, prepositional phrases	Elements of language
1	**A Doggy Hero** Report	to inform	clauses, sentences, conjunctions	personal pronouns			
2	**Battle for the Planets** Narrative	to entertain		noun groups, adjectives, articles	verb group, noun-verb agreement		
3	**The Eagle Has Landed** Newspaper article	to inform	clauses, complex sentences, subordinating conjunctions				commas
4	**The Milky Way** Poem	to entertain to inspire to reflect		noun groups, adjectives, adjectival clauses			main idea, personification, alliteration
5	**A Movie Classic** Review	to respond to persuade			verb groups, modal verbs	modal adverbs	expressing certainty, prefixes, antonyms
6	REVISION						
7	**Through the Doorway** Narrative	to entertain				prepositional phrases, adverbs	orientation, setting, mystery
8	**Valentina Tereshkova** Biography	to inform	clauses	noun groups, pronouns	verbs, verb groups, tense		cohesion
9	**Beyond Earth** Advertisement	to persuade	conjunctions, complex sentences		verb groups		emotive language
10	**Greta Thunberg** Biography	to inform	complex sentences	possessive apostrophes, possessive pronouns		prepositional phrases	subjective and objective language
11	**Amateur Astronomer** Recount	to inform			past tense	adverbs, prepositional phrases	
12	REVISION						
13	**Save Planet Earth** Discussion – talkback radio	to persuade to share opinions	quoted speech		verb groups		quoted speech, persuasive language
14	**The First Astronomers** Report	to inform		singular and plural nouns	verb groups		suffixes
15	**Saving Onega** Narrative	to entertain	clauses, sentences	singular and plural nouns			formal and informal language
16	**Does Life Exist on Other Planets?** Discussion	to persuade to inform to entertain	conjunctions, text connectives				acronyms
17	**Life on Earth** Information report	to inform	statements and questions				subjective and objective language
18	REVISION						

Grammar Rules! Student Book 5 (ISBN 9780655092537) © Tanya Gibb

Unit	Unit name Type of text	Purpose of text	Clauses, sentences, conjunctions, connectives	Nouns, noun groups, pronouns, adjectives	Verbs and verb groups	Adverbs, adverbials, prepositional phrases	Elements of language
19	Save Our Wetlands Speech	to persuade	paragraphs, sentences	noun groups			formal language, synonyms
20	War of the Worlds Review	to persuade	exclamations			adverbs	subjective/objective evaluative language
21	The Sky Emu Report Explanation	to explain	dependent clauses				commas, objective or subjective language
22	Our Earth Poem	to describe to reflect		noun groups		prepositional phrases	figurative language
23	Ecological Footprint Report	to inform	clauses, sentences, conjunctions				Greek and Latin word roots
24	REVISION						
25	Mass Panic – UFO Terrorises City News report	to inform to entertain	reported and quoted speech				emotive language, inclusive language
26	Mars, the Red Planet Report	to inform to describe		adjectives, adjectival phrases, noun groups	verbs		
27	How is the Earth Magnetic? Scientific explanation	to explain			tense, verbs	prepositional phrases	technical terminology
28	Who Needs Science? Speech		connectives		modal verbs	modal adverbs	formal audience, opinions
29	Animal Experimentation is Wrong Debate		sentences and clauses	noun groups			subjective and emotive language
30	REVISION						
31	New Message Text message	to inform to complain		noun groups	verb groups	prepositional phrases	metaphor, simile, idiom, informal language
32	What To Do If An Alien Lands In Your Neighbourhood Instructions	to entertain	commands, conjunctions		tense, auxiliary verbs		tongue-in-cheek humour
33	Escape From Mars Narrative	to entertain		pronouns			first- and third-person narrator
34	The Cost of Space Discussion	to persuade to express opinions	connectives	nouns, noun groups, pronoun reference			cohesion, point of view
35	REVISION						

Unit 1

Clauses, conjunctions, personal pronouns

This text is **informative**. It uses a variety of **sentence** types. The title conveys the writer's opinion of the subject of the text.

A Doggy Hero

The first animal to orbit Earth was a dog named Laika. She was sent to space in a Soviet Union spacecraft named *Sputnik II* in 1957. Laika was a stray dog caught on the streets of Moscow. She was nicknamed 'Muttnik' by the American media. While in space, Laika's heart rate and other vital signs were monitored so that scientists could determine whether it was safe to send humans into orbit. She was harnessed into the spacecraft. The mission was not a return mission, and there was never any intention to bring Laika home. Scientists believe Laika overheated in the spacecraft and died within seven days.

1 Read *A Doggy Hero*. Why is Laika referred to as a hero? ______________________________

____

2 Why was Laika nicknamed Muttnik? ______________________________

____

A **clause** is a unit of meaning that includes a **verb**. A simple sentence is one clause. **Conjunctions** link clauses to form compound and complex sentences.

and so because but or until

3 Circle the **conjunctions** in the sentences below. Underline the **verbs**.

Laika was born in Moscow and she became a very famous Russian dog.

Laika was the first animal to orbit the Earth and she became famous.

Laika was harnessed into the spacecraft but she could reach her food and water.

Laika was the first animal to orbit Earth but she was not the first animal in space.

4 Cross out the incorrect **conjunction** in each example.

Laika overheated (so/or) she died.

Laika died (so/because) *Sputnik II's* heat shield failed.

The dog's name was Laika (but/so) the media called her 'Muttnik'.

5 *A Doggy Hero* has not been written in paragraphs. Draw a dividing line in the text where you think each paragraph should begin.

Grammar Rules! Student Book 5 (ISBN 9780655092537) © Tanya Gibb

A **complex sentence** has two or more clauses. One of the clauses is the **main (independent) clause**. The other clauses in the sentence are **dependent clauses**. They depend on the main clause to fully make sense.

6 Join the sentences using **conjunctions**.

Laika was harnessed into the spacecraft. She couldn't move around.

____

Russian scientists said Laika showed no ill effects from her space flight. She overheated. She died.

____

Laika was a stray dog. No-one objected to sending Laika into space.

____

Laika died in space. She became famous.

____

Personal pronouns replace or refer to **nouns** for people, places, animals and things.

I me you we us he him she her they them it

7 Circle the **personal pronouns** in *A Doggy Hero*.

8 Use a **personal pronoun** from the box to complete each sentence.

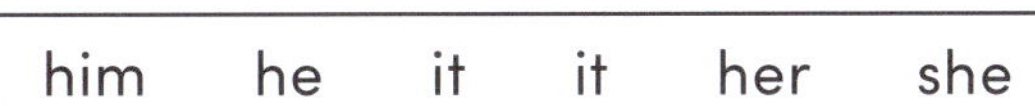

him	he	it	it	her	she

Laika ate her dinner and then __________ licked her lips.

Ralph, the dog, sat under his favourite tree while __________ waited for dinner.

I bought a new lunch box and took __________ to school.

My cat was sick so I took __________ to the vet.

Lena doesn't like it when I tickle __________.

Russell is funny, but don't tell __________ I said so!

9 Rewrite the pair of sentences as one sentence. Use a **conjunction** and a **personal pronoun**.

Elena and Frankie went to the park. Elena and Frankie needed some fresh air.

____

Find out about some other animals that were sent into space, such as spiders, monkeys or mice. Write an **information report**. Use **conjunctions** to connect **clauses** in the sentences. Use **pronouns** to refer to the animals.

Unit 2

Nouns groups, verb groups

This imaginative text is an excerpt from a **narrative**. It uses **noun groups** to describe the **characters** and the **setting**.

Battle for the Planets

In the deep wilderness of space, there lived a peaceful community of Ferlings. The Ferlings were kind, gentle, nomadic creatures. For centuries, they had roamed from planet to planet, constantly under threat of attack by the not-so-friendly Grimlies, of the planet Grima.

One day, a group of Ferlings was collecting sweet, juicy Moonberries and tasty little Jupiternuts when they realised that a gang of huge, fierce Grimlies was moving towards them. They immediately hid behind a nearby rocky outcrop, hoping that they hadn't been seen and waited until they thought the coast was clear before stepping out.

They were wrong! The Grimlies were waiting for them.

1 Narratives are based on one or more **themes**. Read *Battle for the Planets*. Which of the following themes might apply to *Battle for the Planets*?

love hate family survival greed good vs evil courage revenge loyalty death prejudice power freedom war betrayal justice/injustice

Rule **Nouns** name people, places, animals, things and ideas. A **noun group** is a group of words built around a noun to give a more detailed description. A noun group can include an **article** (*a, an, the*), **adjectives** that describe (*spectacular, dangerous*) and an **adjectival phrase** (*the distant planet with the red ocean*).

2 Write a **noun group** for each noun below. Use words from the narrative or your own words.

Ferlings	
space	
Grimlies	
planet	

3 Create an interesting **noun group** for each noun below.

________________________________ friend

________________________________ homework

________________________________ feet

________________________________ dog

________________________________ class

Grammar Rules! Student Book 5 (ISBN 9780655092537) © Tanya Gibb

4 Underline the **personal pronouns** in *Battle for the Planets*. Write the **noun/nouns** that the pronouns refer to. ______________________

5 *Ferlings* and *Grimlies* each begin with a capital letter because they are **proper nouns**. They are the names for creatures from particular places. Write the **proper nouns** for people from the following places.

Australia ____________________

Iraq ____________________

Japan ____________________

Somalia ____________________

Earth ____________________

Germany ____________________

Philippines ____________________

Spain ____________________

Rule

Verbs are words for doing, saying, thinking, feeling and relating.
A **verb group** can include a verb and a helping (auxiliary) verb.
is called *had vanished* *hadn't been seen*
wasn't sleeping *are trying*

6 Underline the **helping (auxiliary) verb** in each sentence. Circle the **verb groups**.

The alien was flying.

The Ferlings are collecting berries.

The star has exploded.

The children were giggling.

The Grimly was shouting.

Joseph is jumping.

Rule

A **plural noun** needs a matching **auxiliary verb**. *Grimlies were coming.*
A **singular noun** needs a matching **auxiliary verb**. *A Grimly was coming.*
Collective nouns are singular. *The gang was coming.*

7 Circle the **collective nouns** in *Battle for the Planets*.

8 Circle the **helping (auxiliary) verb** that matches each underlined **noun**.

A group of Grimlies (are/is) setting a trap.

The dogs (were/was) running through the park.

A pack of wolves (was/were) hunting.

The seagulls (is/are) flying overhead.

The boy (is/are) going to be late.

The pod of whales (are/is) moving north past Moreton Bay.

The herd (is/are) heading for the river.

Try it yourself!

Write an ending for the **narrative** *Battle for the Planets*. Or write a **narrative** of your own about creatures from outer space. Create interesting descriptions of characters and settings using **noun groups** with **adjectives**.

Unit 3

Clauses, conjunctions, commas

This newspaper article uses **complex sentences** to convey the information.

Daily News, 20 July 1969

THE EAGLE HAS LANDED

An estimated 700 million people around the world watched in awe as the lunar module *Eagle* landed in the dusty Sea of Tranquillity, and its Commander, Neil Armstrong, and Lunar Module Pilot, Edwin 'Buzz' Aldrin, stepped onto the surface of the Moon, while the Command Module Pilot, Michael Collins, orbited above them.

Apollo 11 was launched on 16th July from the Kennedy Space Center in Florida. The astronauts spent two and a half hours on the surface taking photographs, collecting rocks and drilling for core samples.

Rule

Conjunctions can join a **dependent clause** to a **main (independent) clause.**

while since after when before if unless although therefore because as as if

1 Read *The Eagle has Landed*. The first paragraph is a single sentence with four **clauses**. Mark where each clause begins.
Hint! Look for the **conjunctions** *as*, *and* and *while*. They function to link clauses.
Also remember, a clause must contain a **verb**. Underline the verbs.

2 Write the **clauses** from question 1 as four **simple sentences**.

____

____

____

____

3 Mark the **clauses** in the sentences. Hint! Find the **conjunctions** and the **verbs** first.

Over half a billion people watched televisions around the world as Armstrong climbed down the ladder of the lunar module and took his first footstep on the Moon's surface.

Aldrin joined Armstrong on the lunar surface and described the moonscape as 'magnificent desolation'.

The astronauts were trained to control all equipment and land the module themselves if the computers broke down.

Grammar Rules! Student Book 5 (ISBN 9780655092537) © Tanya Gibb

4 Use **conjunctions** to join each group of **simple sentences** to create **complex sentences**.

The *Daily News* sold out on 20th July. The paper had to be reprinted. Everyone wanted souvenir copies of the paper.

____

____

Armstrong and Aldrin walked on the Moon. Collins orbited above the Moon. The team on Earth watched excitedly.

____

____

5 Every **clause** (or simple sentence) needs a **verb**. Circle the **verb** in each row.

watched	lunar	ship	astronaut
Moon	dust	rock	landed
newspaper	stepped	daily	space centre
Michael	orbited	while	surface

6 Tick the box for each row below that is a **sentence**. Add sentence punctuation where it is needed.

the astronauts collected materials	☐
rocks, soil and dust	☐
they reprinted the paper	☐
souvenir copies of the paper	☐
the Kennedy Space Center	☐

Rule

Commas are punctuation marks that are used to separate
- words in a list (*apples, bananas and oranges*)
- a phrase in a sentence (*After lunch, we went for a walk.*)
- a dependent clause in a sentence where the dependent clause comes first (*While orbiting above the moon, Collins did safety checks.*).

7 Add **commas** to these sentences to make the meaning clear.

During their walk Armstrong and Aldrin collected rocks soil and dust from the surface.

Because of their Moon mission Neil Armstrong Buzz Aldrin and Michael Collins are very famous.

During his time in orbit Collins checked his instruments and equipment.

After the worker was injured workplace rules have become more strict.

The astronauts took photos collected rocks and drilled for core samples.

Choose a famous event in history to research. Write a news article about it. How did people react to the event at the time? Include statements from witnesses and experts.

This poem uses **noun groups** and **adjectives** to describe the Milky Way galaxy.

The Milky Way

A spiral galaxy.
A dusty, gassy, pinwheel
with a massive black hole
at its centre,
surrounded by 200 billion
stars.
Some in clusters.
Some young.
Some old.
Some brighter than our Sun.
Some obscured by space dust
but
still luminous,
spiralling in the night sky,
strung together by gravity.
A hungry galaxy,
consuming
other galaxies
and growing
over time
– billions of years of time.
An ancient galaxy,
nearly as old as the universe itself.
So vast.
So much unknown.
A pinwheel in space
holding our solar system,
our Earth,
our sun
on just one arm.

Rule A **noun group** can include **adjectives** that quantify or tell number (*one* galaxy, *some* authors, *many* people), **determiners** that point out (*this* space suit, *those* stars) and nouns that **classify** other nouns (*apple* pie).

1 Read *The Milky Way*. Underline the **adjectives** that describe.

2 In *The Milky Way*, circle three **nouns** used to classify other nouns in the noun group.

3 Find and write two **noun groups** in *The Milky Way* that include words that quantify or tell number.

____

4 What is the **main idea** in the poem? Hint! This is the idea the poet wants you to accept or understand.

____

How do you think the poet feels about the Milky Way?

____

5 **Personification** is when human qualities are given to non-human things. What human qualities does the poet give to the Milky Way?

____

6 Some poems use alliteration. Recite *The Milky Way*. Did you notice any letter sound that is used more frequently than other sounds? What is it? ______________

Grammar Rules! Student Book 5 (ISBN 9780655092537) © Tanya Gibb

A **noun group** can include a **possessive adjective** to show possession.

my our your his her their its

7 Complete the sentence with **possessive adjectives**.

The Milky Way has gravity that holds __________ solar system on __________ arm.

8 Use a word from the box to show **possession** in each **noun group**.

my	our	your	his	her	their	its

They ran to catch __________ bus.

Give me __________ hand while we cross the road.

I'll lend you __________ compass to take on the hike.

Ask Giselle if you can borrow __________ ruler.

The Earth rotates on __________ axis.

Mr Webster has forgotten __________ keys.

'Look, Dane! There's __________ base camp,' said Zoe.

Adjectival clauses help to build detailed descriptions. Use words such as *who, whom, whose, which* or *that* to join an adjectival clause to a **main clause**.

The koala that had a sore leg climbed to the top of the tree.

I met the teacher who will take over from Ms Willis.

8 Circle the **adjectival clauses** and underline the **nouns** they describe.

We only buy cherries that are grown in Australia.

Investors who have an interest in space are funding the flight.

Where are the instructions that we need to follow?

The novel, which is science fiction, will keep you intrigued.

Children for whom reading is difficult will be given extra tutoring.

The teachers were very proud of students who achieved improved results.

Our sun, whose warmth lights our days, is halfway through its life.

Planets that we can see in the night sky include Venus, Mars, Saturn and Jupiter.

I'm looking for a planet that looks golden in colour.

Write a poem that uses **adjectives** and extended **noun groups** to describe the topic. Use personification, alliteration and other poetic devices to help readers imagine or form a mental picture of the topic.

Unit 5

Verb groups, modal verbs and adverbs, prefixes

This persuasive text is a **response**. It uses **thinking verbs** and **saying verbs** to give opinions.

A Movie Classic

I recently saw an old movie on television. It was called *E.T. the Extra-Terrestrial*. Mum suggested I watch it with her. It was made in 1982, the year Mum was born. Mum told me that she saw the movie with her parents when she was ten and had really loved it. She remembered feeling really sad about the little alien, E.T. She also remembers thinking that the scientists were certainly planning to experiment on E.T. and kill him. They should have tried to help E.T. go home. Watching the movie together last week, we both cheered when E.T. managed to escape.

E.T. the Extra-Terrestrial is a science fiction adventure that the whole family should definitely watch. Even though it was made decades ago, I believe it still has a relevant message for Earthlings today.

Rule A **verb group** can include two verbs that contribute equally to the meaning (*remembered seeing*).

1 Read *A Movie Classic*. Circle the three **saying verbs**.

2 Write five **saying verbs** that you could use in your own writing.

3 Underline the five **thinking verbs** or **verb groups** in *A Movie Classic*.

4 Write five **thinking verbs** or **verb groups** that you could use in your own writing.

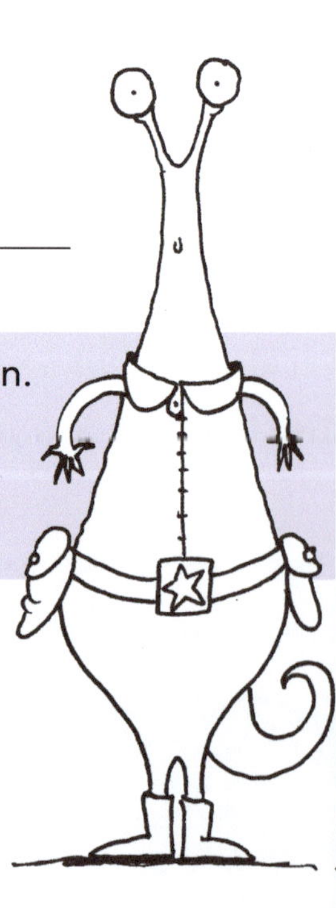

Rule A **verb group** can express degrees of possibility, certainty or obligation.

will go *might go* *must go* *won't go* *can't go*

Some adverbs help to express certainty.

definitely will go *probably won't go* *will not go*

5 Circle all the **verbs** and **verb groups** below.

'I really didn't enjoy *E.T.*,' announced Sanjay. 'The special effects are too basic. I definitely prefer the *Avatar* movies. They have amazing visual effects. I saw *Avatar: The Way of Water*. I can't believe the technology the film makers needed to develop so they could create that movie.'

Grammar Rules! Student Book 5 (ISBN 9780655092537) ©Tanya Gibb

6 In *A Movie Classic*, find and write two verb groups that include **adverbs** that express possibility, certainty or obligation.

____

7 Find and copy a **complex sentence** from *A Movie Classic* that uses two **conjunctions**.

____

____

8 If you desperately needed to go to the toilet in class, tick the line you would use with your teacher.

I might need to go to the toilet.

I possibly should go to the toilet.

Maybe you'll let me go to the toilet.

I really must go to the toilet!

9 Underline the **verbs** and **verb groups**. Circle the **conjunctions**.

'I really loved *E.T.*,' responded Kate. 'I generally don't like science fiction movies because I prefer realistic movies, but *E.T.* was special.'

10 Complete each sentence with an **adverb** that expresses certainty or obligation

Mum ________________ agrees that *E.T.* is a movie classic.

I ________________ love watching old movies.

We should ________________ make a movie ourselves!

I will ________________ watch *Avatar: The Way of Water* again.

Rule

A **prefix** is a word part added to the beginning of a word to change its meaning. Many prefixes create **antonyms** or opposites.

use – reuse *information – misinformation* *decided – undecided*

11 Add a **prefix** to create new words. Use each prefix once.

ir	un	dis	bi	over	semi	non	mid	sub	pre	auto	de

respect ____________ responsible ____________ use ____________ mobile ____________

annual ____________ specific ____________ night ____________ natural ____________

marine ____________ school ____________ final ____________ hydrated ____________

Try it yourself!

Write a **response** to a movie you have seen. Include **thinking verbs**. Use **verbs** and **adverbs** to help express your opinions.

Revision

1 Use a **conjunction** from the box to connect each pair of **simple sentences**.

and	so	but	because	or

It is cold in space. I need to wear a jacket.

____

I need to wear a coat. I don't want to get cold.

____

I could put my jacket on. I could just go in my T-shirt.

____

I'll wear a jacket. I'll wear gloves.

____

I could take my coat. I don't want to carry it around.

____

2 Use a **personal pronoun** from the box to complete each sentence.

he	her	she	it

The scientist washed her hands before ________ put on her gloves.

Roger, the cat, sat on his favourite chair while ________ waited for dinner.

I borrowed Jacob's skateboard and rode ________ after dinner.

Sofia was hungry so I fed ________ a snack.

3 Circle the correct **verb** form for each sentence.

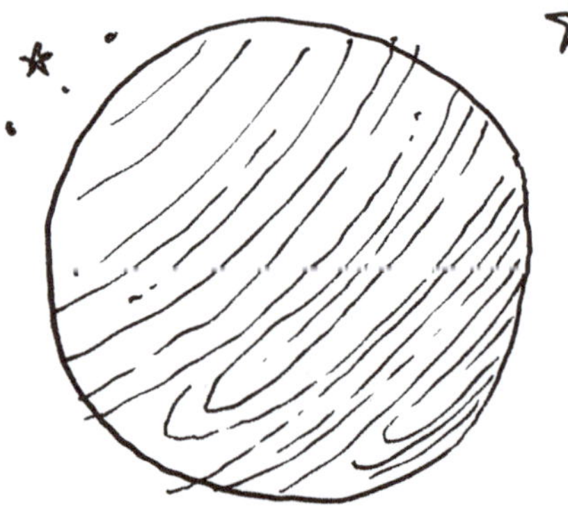

The pancakes (were/was) delicious.

They (was/were) hoping to earn extra pocket money.

The fish (were/was) swimming around their tank.

The seagull (is/are) trying to steal my sandwich.

The team (is/are) blasting off to Jupiter.

The shark (are/is) a harmless grey nurse.

4 Add **commas** in the correct places.

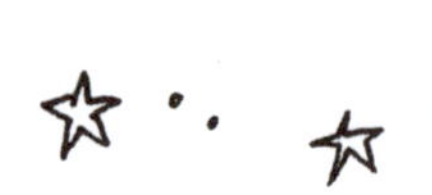

Ben bought a jumper shorts socks and a pair of jeans.

During the television commercial Dad made a snack of cookies milk cheese and crackers.

Even though it was raining the soccer team practised corners penalty kicks and shootouts.

5 Write an interesting extended **noun group** for each noun.

______________________________ spaceship

______________________________ pie

______________________________ boots

______________________________ mission

6 Circle the **verb group** in each sentence.

Our class will be returning from the museum at 3 pm.

Mel won't be able to participate in the Aussie Bird Count this year.

Yulia has definitely completed her spelling homework.

Maxim might be able to meet with us on Sunday.

Selina couldn't remember watching the movie.

Lane quickly made pikelets for morning tea.

7 Use a word from the box to show **possession** in each **noun group**.

their	your	my	our	its

You need to complete __________ homework before bedtime.

They planted a lemon myrtle tree in __________ garden.

'Take __________ umbrella with you,' suggested Molly.

The spider is shedding __________ exoskeleton.

'Wake up, Chloe! This is __________ bus,' announced Zac.

8 Use a word from the box to join each pair of simple sentences. Write the new sentences.

who	that	that	which

Eden normally answers the phone. She is sick.

____

Here is the pizza. The pizza has ham and pineapple topping.

____

Possums lived in the tree. The tree burned down in the fire.

____

The astronaut could not wear the spacesuit. It had a hole.

____

9 Write a sentence that tells exactly what you think about homework. Use **verbs** and **adverbs** that express certainty.

____

____

Unit 7

Prepositional phrases, adverbs

Through the Doorway

Ronnie looked out her window at the blinding light that was coming from the neighbourhood park. She wondered what it could be. She messaged her friend Lila to meet her there, then crept out the back door without a sound. She wheeled her bike onto the street, then climbed on and headed down the road to the park.

When she got there, Lila was already waiting, and Ronnie was astonished to see that all the light was coming from a small shoe-sized box. She knelt down next to it and lifted the lid. Inside was a remote control. Ronnie picked it up. A red light in the centre started flashing.

Without thinking, Ronnie pushed the red button. Bang! An ear-splitting noise shattered the night. She jumped back quickly, and before her eyes, the remote turned into a gigantic doorway. Ronnie peered through.

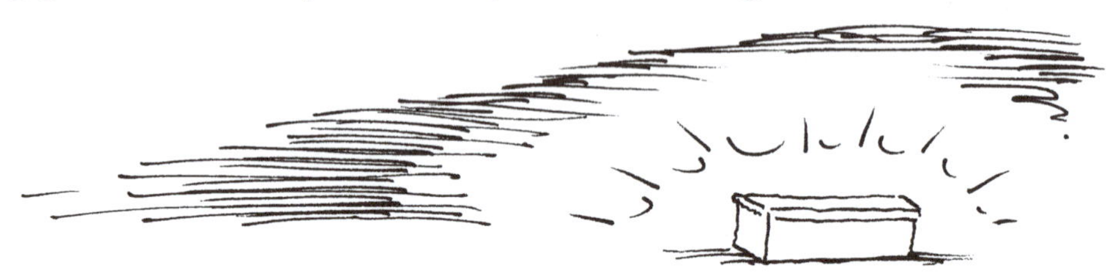

This is the orientation from a **narrative**. It introduces the **main character** and a **complication** or mystery for the character to resolve.

Rule

A **prepositional phrase** is a preposition linked to a **noun** or **noun group**.

They can tell place (where). *near the stove* *under the bed* *in the kitchen cupboard*

They can tell time (when). *during the night* *after the storm* *before sunrise*

They can tell manner (how). *with complete dread* *in a funny way* *without her shoes*

1 Read *Through the Doorway*. Underline the **prepositional phrases** that tell place (where).

2 Find and copy two **prepositional phrases** in *Through the Doorway* that tell manner (how).

____

3 Finish each sentence with a **prepositional phrase** that tells place (where).

Victoria walked ______________________________.

The cat sat ______________________________.

The galaxy was located ______________________________.

We watched the fireworks ______________________________.

4 What does the **title** of the story imply?

____

Grammar Rules! Student Book 5 (ISBN 9780655092537) © Tanya Gibb

Tip

Adverbs add meaning to a **verb**, **adjective** or another **adverb**.
They can tell manner (how). *slowly*
They can tell time (when). *tomorrow*
They can tell place (where). *here*
An **adverb group** is a group of words that does the job of an adverb.
He walked back and forth.

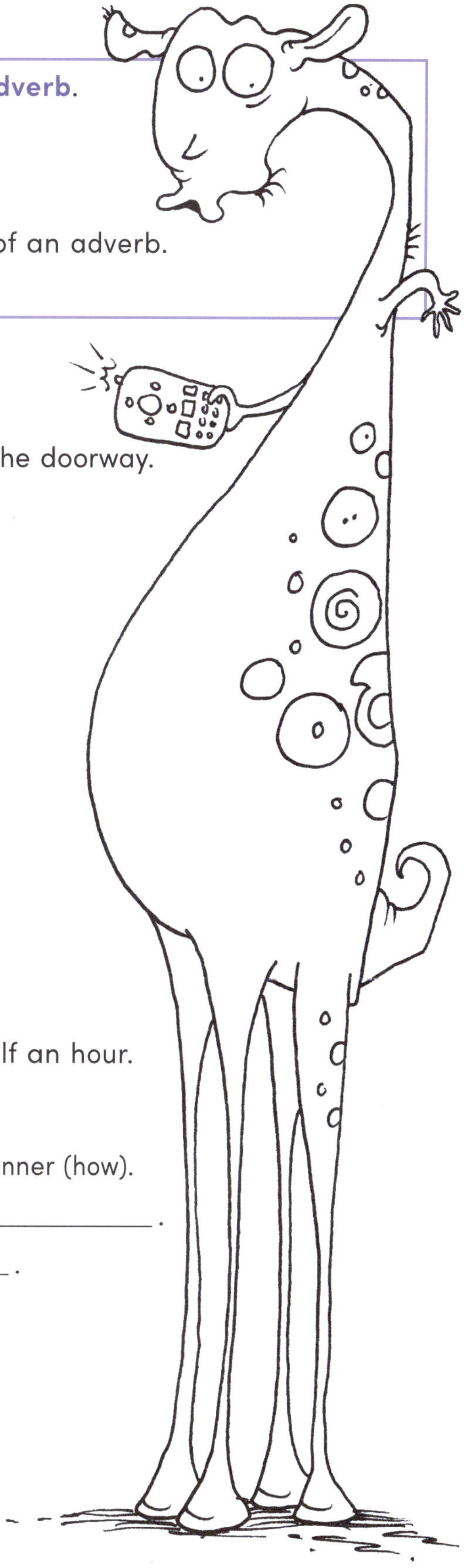

5 Underline the **adverb** in each sentence. Circle the **verb** it modifies.

Ronnie pushed the button recklessly.

Ronnie is an inquisitive person and she peered cautiously through the doorway.

Ronnie looked inquisitively at the remote.

Ronnie could see clearly through the well-lit doorway.

Being a clever girl, Ronnie decided to approach carefully.

The remote buzzed loudly.

6 Use an **adverb** or **adverb group** from the box to complete each sentence. The adverb or adverb group will tell time (when). Use a capital letter if the adverb begins a sentence.

last night	tomorrow	soon	later	before

I will walk to the shop ________________.

________________ we went to the movies.

We will go swimming ________________.

________________ we go to bed, we can watch television for half an hour.

I'll finish reading my book ________________.

7 Complete each sentence with an **adverb** ending in *-ly* that tells manner (how).

I walked _____________. I ran _____________. Dad sang _____________.

You need to work _____________. My sister ate _____________.

8 Complete each sentence with an **adverb** that tells place (where).

here	there	above	below	inside

The key is on the shelf _____________.

Look _____________ the window. I ran _____________.

Tracey is _____________. I saw the bird _____________.

Try it yourself!

Write a narrative titled *Through the Doorway*. You could continue the story started in this unit or create your own magic doorway. Use **prepositional phrases** and **adverbs** to set the scene. Ask a peer to help edit your story.

Unit 8

Verb groups, tense, clauses, noun groups, pronouns

Valentina Tereshkova

The first woman in space was a Soviet cosmonaut, Valentina Tereshkova, in 1963 onboard *Vostok 6*. She was 26 years of age.

Valentina had left school at age 17 so that she could help support the family. She continued her education via correspondence school and she learned to parachute. She started a parachuting club at the textile factory where she worked. She was chosen for the cosmonaut training program because of her parachuting expertise.

The Soviet Union had sent the first man, Yuri Gagarin, and the first dog, Laika, into space and it was keen to send the first woman into space, ahead of the Americans.

Valentina spent three days in orbit and she landed safely back on Earth.

This text is written in the past **tense** to tell about events that have occurred. Each **clause** begins with a **noun/noun group** or **pronoun**.

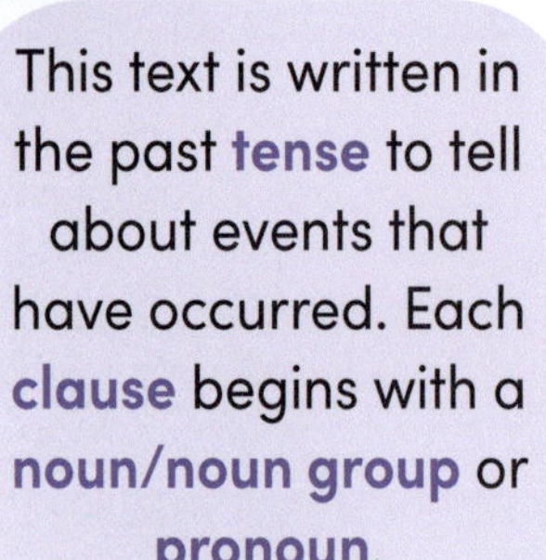

Rule

Verbs anchor events in time. This is called **tense**.
Past tense: went, have been, did go
Present tense: is going, goes
Future tense: will go, might go
Auxiliary (helping) verbs (*is, was, are, has, have, had*) and **suffixes** (*-ing, -ed, -en, -t, -d*) help show tense.

1 Read *Valentina Tereshkova*. Circle all the **verbs** and **verb groups**. What kinds of verbs did you find?

____

2 Use different **doing verbs** in each sentence.

Valentina ____________ three days in orbit and ____________ safely home.
Valentina ____________ three days in orbit and ____________ safely home.
Valentina ____________ three days in orbit and ____________ safely home.

3 Use a **relating verb** in each space.

deserves	is	being	contributed	symbolises

Valentina ______________ famous for ______________ the first woman in space.
Valentina ______________ a medal for bravery.
Valentina ______________ to the Russian space program.
She ______________ the role of women in science.

Grammar Rules! Student Book 5 (ISBN 9780655092537) © Tanya Gibb

4 Use a **verb group** from the box in each sentence.

are destroyed	can reach	have totally evaporated	was discovered

Comets ____________________ when they approach too close to the Sun.

Pluto ____________________ in 1930.

Wind speeds on Saturn ____________________ 1800 kilometres per hour.

Prehistoric oceans on Venus ____________________________.

5 Write any six **prepositional phases** used in *Valentina Tereshkova*.

____

____

Rule The types of words used at the beginning of each sentence in a text signal how the text is developing. Informative texts often use **nouns**, **noun groups** and **pronouns** at the beginning of **clauses** or **sentences**.

6 Underline the **nouns**, **noun groups** and **pronouns** at the beginning of each sentence in *Valentina Tereshkova*. Write the one that does not refer to Valentina.

____

7 In each paragraph below, circle the first word or word group in each **sentence**.

Magpies are magnificent birds. They can be found just about all over Australia.
Adult magpies are black and white in colour. They sing a beautiful warbling song.
Magpies are quite territorial and magpie families stay together.

Which kinds of words did you circle? ______________________________________

Mercury is the closest planet to the Sun. It is also the smallest planet. Mercury has many large craters on its surface. It has an iron core. Mercury can reach temperatures of 430°C.

Which kinds of words did you circle? ______________________________________

8 Write a summary of the important points made in *Valentina Tereshkova*.

____

____

____

Choose a famous person from history who interests you. Search the internet to find appropriate material and create a biography for the person. Use **noun groups** and **pronouns** for the person at the beginning of sentences to ensure your text is cohesive. Create a multimodal presentation for the class.

Unit 9

Conjunctions, complex sentences, emotive language

Beyond Earth

See the earth from 110 kilometres.

Travel into space – and back – on the new Beyond Earth spaceship, *Petrel 1*.

- Minimum training required – involving simulator experience of zero gravity.
- Unparalleled safety features.
- Fully compliant with the highest international safety standards.

Book your out-of-this-world trip NOW! Seats are limited!

Contact Beyond Earth now. Your exciting adventure awaits.

beyondearth@spaceorg.com

This **advertisement** uses **emotive language** to persuade readers to take action.

Tip Using a **doing verb** first in a sentence indicates a **command**. The advertisers are telling readers what to do.

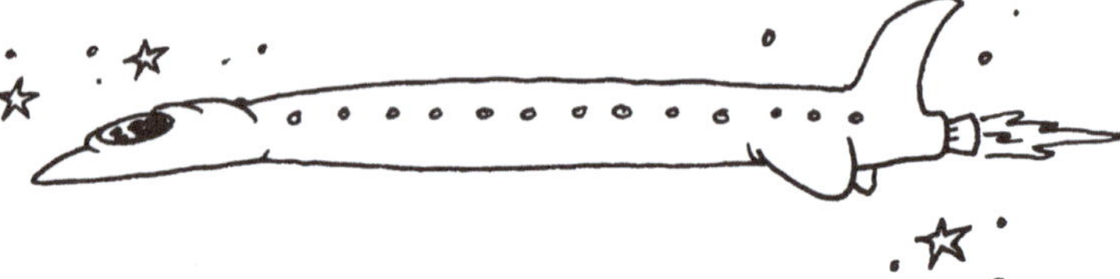

1 Read *Beyond Earth*. Circle the **doing verbs** used in the **commands**.

Tip **Emotive language** is used to evoke an emotional response from readers/listeners. It is used in advertising to persuade. It can include **adjectives** (*hideous, spectacular*), **noun groups** (*fantastic opportunity*) and **verbs** (*experience weightlessness*), as well as **commands** (*Don't miss out!*).

2 Write the words and phrases in *Beyond Earth* that are **emotive** and **persuasive**.

____

____

3 Write the noun groups that include **possessive adjectives** in *Beyond Earth*.

____

Who do these possessive adjectives address? ______________________________

4 Does the **advertisement** *Beyond Earth* persuade you to want to take a trip into space? Explain.

____

____

Grammar Rules! Student Book 5 (ISBN 9780655092537) © Tanya Gibb

Positive and negative statements can both express certainty.

positive *I can come tomorrow.*

negative *I cannot come tomorrow.*

5 Complete the table.

Definitely positive	Somewhat positive	Somewhat negative	Definitely negative
He's hungry.			
She heard.			
			It will not rain.
			You must not stop.
	They might be ready.		

6 Add a **conjunction** from the box to each complex sentence.

Since	Before	Unless	While	Although	When

____________ prices drop, few people will be able to afford a space flight.

____________ she returned from space, Mary Webber said she'd save up for another trip.

____________ returning to Earth in June, *Petrel 1* has been undergoing safety checks.

____________ they can join the crew, astronauts undertake health checks.

____________ it's expensive, space tourists say it's worth it.

____________ he was in space, Dimitri Hall realised how tiny earth is.

7 Imagine you are a passenger who has been on the space flight advertised in *Beyond Earth*. Rewrite the advertisement as a recommendation to potential passengers.
Use **emotive words** and **personal pronouns** (*I, we, you*).

Create an advertisement for a holiday on Mars, a walk on the Moon or something else that you think you can sell. Use **commands** and **emotive language** to persuade.

Unit 10

Subjective/objective language, possessive apostrophes, possessive pronouns

This text is a **biography**. It uses **prepositional phrases** to sequence events in time.

Greta Thunberg

Greta Thunberg is a climate change activist. She was born in Sweden in 2003, and she became concerned about climate change and the future of the Earth when she was just eight years of age. Between the ages of 8 and 15, Greta grew more and more concerned about climate change.

In 2018, when Greta was 15, she decided that instead of going to school, she would sit outside the Swedish Parliament House with a protest sign that said 'SCHOOL STRIKE FOR CLIMATE'. She gained media attention with her silent protest, and before long she had inspired an international climate protest movement.

Greta's actions show that every single person can make a difference to the world and that you are never too young to start standing up for your beliefs.

Rule

An **apostrophe** can show possession. An apostrophe with a **noun** shows that something belongs to that noun.

singular noun → add *'s*	*Earth's future*
plural noun ending in *s* → add *'*	*the astronauts' achievements*
plural noun not ending in *s* → add *'s*	*the women's voyage*

1 Read *Greta Thunberg*. Circle the **apostrophe** that shows possession.

2 Rewrite each phrase using an **apostrophe** to show possession.

the spaceship of the cosmonaut → ____________________

the training of the pilots → ____________________

the space boots belonging to the children → ____________________

Rule

Possessive pronouns show possession. *his hers theirs yours mine ours*

The telescope is his. *The Moon rock is mine.*

3 Use a **possessive pronoun** from the box to complete each sentence.

mine
ours
yours
his
hers
theirs

Greta received an award. The award is ____________.

We should protect the earth. The responsibility is ____________.

The recycling bin belongs to John and Jenny. It is ____________.

The cat belongs to him. It is ____________.

The dog belongs to you. It is ____________.

The book belongs to me. It is ____________.

Grammar Rules! Student Book 5 (ISBN 9780655092537) © Tanya Gibb

4 In *Greta Thunberg*, underline the **nouns**, **noun groups** and **pronouns** that refer to Greta throughout the text.

5 Rewrite each pair of sentences as a single complex sentence, using one of the **pronouns** from the box.

who	whose	that	which

Yuri Gagarin's spaceship was called *Vostok 1*. Yuri Gagarin was the first person to orbit the Earth.

____

Yuri Gagarin was a famous Soviet cosmonaut. Yuri Gagarin died on a training flight.

____

The spaceship took the Russian cosmonaut into space in 1961. The spaceship was called *Vostok 1.*

____

The spaceship circled the Earth at 27,400 kilometres per hour. Yuri Gagarin flew the spaceship.

____

Language can be **objective** and unbiased. *a 30-minute spelling test*
Language can be **subjective** and biased. *a challenging spelling test*

6 Underline the **subjective** words in each sentence.

Cows produce climate-wrecking methane gas.
I love the rain.
Greta Thunberg has given inspirational speeches around the world.
Sweet, juicy tomatoes are inexpensive at the moment.

7 Rewrite the sentences by adding in the missing punctuation markers.

in 2019, greta thunberg told world leaders at the united nations climate action summit that they were failing children

____

____

Prepare a speech to present to your class. Choose a person you admire. Do some research and write their biography. Use **subjective language** that shows your opinion of the person. Summarise the information on cue cards. Rehearse and then present your speech to the class.

Unit 11

Past tense, adverbs, prepositional phrases

This informative text is a **recount**. It uses **adverbs** and **prepositional phrases** to tell when events happened.

Amateur Astronomer

During the last school holidays, my family and I drove to Dubbo Zoo in country New South Wales. On the way, we stopped for a night in Coonabarabran where there is the Siding Spring Observatory and the Skywatch Observatory, which we visited.

The Skywatch Observatory has four telescopes outside on a viewing platform. Through the telescopes we saw Venus and Jupiter, the Great Nebula in Orion, the Tarantula Nebula and Omega Centauri. The night was crystal clear and the sky looked amazing.

Apparently you can look at the surface of the Sun using a solar filter on a telescope, if you visit during the day, but we didn't have time. We had to get to the zoo and that's a whole other story.

By Cate

1 Read *Amateur Astronomer*. What is an amateur astronomer?

____

2 What is the writer's opinion of the events in *Amateur Astronomer*?

____

3 Find the **contraction** in *Amateur Astronomer*. Write its full form. Hint! A contraction is a combination or two or more words. An apostrophe marks the place of any letters left out. ______________

4 Write four **prepositional phrases** in *Amateur Astronomer* that tell when events occurred (time).

____

____

5 Write four **prepositional phrases** in *Amateur Astronomer* that tell where events occurred (place).

____

____

____

Some **verbs** have more than one **past tense form**.
The form to use depends on which, if any, **auxiliary verb** is also used.
I ate. *I have eaten.* *I did eat.*

Grammar Rules! Student Book 5 (ISBN 9780655092537) © Tanya Gibb

6 Write the **verb** forms to show **past tense**.

Base form	Past tense with auxiliary	Past tense without auxiliary
travel	I have travelled.	I travelled.
look	I have	I
visit	I had	I
steal	The dog had	It
eat	I had been	I
grow	I did	I
think	I was	I
see	I have	I

7 Write a sentence for each of these **adverbs** that tells about an event in the past.

yesterday previously later overnight afterwards

8 Write a sentence for each of these **prepositional phrases** that tells about an event in the past.

after lunch during the night an hour on Tuesday

Create an **imaginative recount** for a place. It could be anywhere in the world or in outer space. Imagine you have been there. What did you do and see? Use **past tense verbs** as well as **adverbs** and **prepositional phrases** for time and place.

Unit 12

Revision

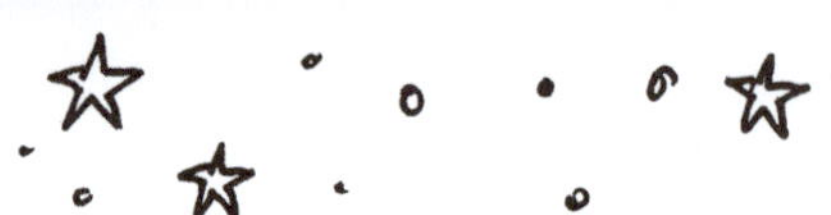

1 Complete each sentence with at least two **adverbs** or **prepositional phrases** that tell place (where).

The asteroid belt was located ______________________________.

We had a party ______________________________.

______________________________ the UFO hovered.

Nuala trudged ______________________________.

The cosmonaut stood ______________________________.

2 Complete each sentence with an **adverb** or **prepositional phrase** that tells time (when).

I dashed to the shop to buy milk ____________________.

____________________ I missed my tuba lesson.

My sister burped loudly ____________________.

Will you sleep at my house one day ____________________?

Can't I just do it ____________________?

3 Underline the **adverb** that tells manner (how) in each sentence. Write the **verb** each adverb modifies.

The goose honked loudly. ____________________

The television star smiled brightly. ____________________

The student giggled wildly. ____________________

The teacher sighed patiently. ____________________

The doorbell chimed annoyingly. ____________________

4 Use a **possessive pronoun** from the box to complete each sentence.

theirs	his	hers	ours

Billy owns the bike. It is __________.

The toy belongs to my sister. The toy is __________.

Jeff and Judy own the car. It is __________.

The computer belongs to us. It is __________.

5 Circle the **word/word group** used to begin each sentence.

An alien spaceship landed in the park. An alien slid out. Its head was the shape of a pumpkin. It had eyes on stalks. It had tentacles for arms. It said, '#@*!!!!!###oOoOO.'

6 Rewrite each phrase using an **apostrophe** to show possession.

the car belonging to Mum ______________________________

the flowers belonging to the teacher ______________________________

the warbling of the magpies ______________________________

Grammar Rules! Student Book 5 (ISBN 9780655092537) © Tanya Gibb

7 Join the **simple sentences** to create **complex sentences**. Use a **pronoun** from the box.

who	whose	that	which

The house was owned by Jack's great, great grandpa. The house was built in 1901.

____

My sister has a cat named Bozo. My sister loves her cat.

____

My aunt writes books. She is very famous.

____

The bananas were overripe. They were used in the cake.

____

8 Rewrite each set of sentences as a **complex sentence**.

I took the bike back to the shop. Mum bought me the bike. The bike had a crack in the shaft.

____

My dad is putting in a basketball hoop. I can practise for the finals. The finals are coming up in July.

____

9 Circle the more certain statement in each pair.

Caleb might join the team.	Caleb shouldn't join the team.
Jason probably has the flu.	Jason possibly has the flu.
We'll collect the cans for recycling.	We should collect the cans for recycling.
Lulu needs antibiotics.	Lulu should probably have antibiotics.
Fraser ought to eat more vegetables.	Fraser must eat more vegetables.

10 Write **subjective** or **objective** after each sentence.

Bananas are expensive this week. ____________________

Bananas cost more per kilo than apples at my local store today. ____________________

11 Write **past tense verb** forms.

Base form	Past tense with auxiliary	Past tense without auxiliary
put	I have put	I put
break	I have	I
keep	I have	I
ask	I have	I
write	I have	I
blow	I have	I

Unit 13

Verb groups, quoted speech

This persuasive text is a **discussion** on talkback radio. **Thinking verbs** are used to present the **points of view**.

Save Planet Earth

Announcer: Good morning, listeners. Today we are discussing climate change. Go ahead caller 1.

Caller 1: I think the world's nations must do more to prevent further climate change because if we don't protect the Earth, we have no future.

Announcer: Do you have something to say about that caller 2?

Caller 2: Yes, I absolutely agree with the previous caller, but also, Australia really must help other nations mitigate the impacts of climate change. Some Pacific Islands will be uninhabitable before long. Australia has benefited from fossil fuels and worsened climate change while developing countries have not, and they are suffering more than us.

Caller 3: I disagree with those last comments. I don't think Australia should be doing more to help other nations cope with climate change because we have our own problems.

Announcer: Well it seems that our listeners all agree that climate change is a huge threat but there's no agreement about the extent of Australia's responsibility to help other nations. We'll continue the discussion tomorrow from 6 am.

1 Read *Save Planet Earth*. Find and underline three **verb groups** that express opinions with certainty.

Tip: Remember the rule on page 16.

2 Write definitions for the following terms used in *Save Planet Earth*. Use a dictionary.

climate change ______________________________

fossil fuel ______________________________

mitigate ______________________________

uninhabitable ______________________________

prevent ______________________________

3 Do your think the announcer's summing up of the discussion is correct? Explain.

____

____

Grammar Rules! Student Book 5 (ISBN 9780655092537) © Tanya Gibb

4 Rewrite the sentences to express the opinions more forcefully and persuasively.

We might be able to do something to help Pacific Islands nations.

____

Australia is possibly not doing enough about climate change.

____

Some countries could do more to try to prevent pollution.

____

Some people say that Australia has a poor environmental record.

____

5 Number each group of sentences from 1 to 4. 1 is for least certain and 4 is for most certain.

☐ It will definitely rain tomorrow.	☐ I'm not going.
☐ It could possibly rain tomorrow.	☐ I'm definitely never going.
☐ It will rain tomorrow.	☐ I probably won't go.
☐ It's likely to rain tomorrow.	☐ I don't think I'll go.

Rule

Quoted speech is the speech someone has said. It is written inside **quotation marks**.

'I'll take the batteries to be recycled,' said Lucia.

6 Rewrite each sentence with correct punctuation. Hint! The names of organisations are proper nouns.

in 1971 the united nations secretary general called earth a fragile spaceship said lars

____

we gave yuriy a telescope for his birthday said victoria

____

my teacher read us a quote by u thant about earth day said bing

____

did you know that u in burmese means mister asked lauren

____

imagine travelling on a space flight to mars said phoebe

____

Choose a topic of interest to your classmates. Interview classmates to find out their opinion. Write your findings as a **discussion**. Record all points of view using **thinking verbs**. Write a concluding statement that expresses your own opinion.

Unit 14

Verb groups, plural nouns, suffixes, prefixes

This text is **informative**. The first **paragraph** introduces the topic. **Dot points** help to organise the information.

The First Astronomers

Astronomy is the study of space, objects in space and the universe. Australia's First Nations peoples have been observers of space for more than 65,000 years. They were the world's first astronomers.

First Nations Australians have used the Sun, Moon and stars:

- for navigation
- as calendars to anticipate changing seasons and for predicting the weather
- to tell when to hold particular ceremonies
- for predicting animal behaviours, such as where and when animals would be available for food, including using the moon's phases to predict tides and to tell when the best time would be to catch fish
- to know when to harvest plants or when plants would be available for food and medicine.

1 Read *The First Astronomers*. Circle the **verbs/verb groups** in paragraph 1.

2 *Astronomy* and *astronomers* begin with 'astro'. Use a dictionary to find three other words beginning with 'astro' that relate to the stars and space. Write their definitions.

____

____

____

Many **singular nouns** add *s* or *-es* to form plurals. Some nouns form **plurals** in a different way. *phenomenon – phenomena*

3 Write five **plural nouns** used in *The First Astronomers*.

____

4 Write the **plural forms** of these nouns.

millennium ____________	medium ____________
focus ____________	fungus ____________
cactus ____________	octopus ____________
hippopotamus ____________	axis ____________
crisis ____________	louse ____________
index ____________	appendix ____________

Some **suffixes** change the grammatical form of a word.

I will protect koalas because it's important. The protection of koalas is important.

verb group — noun group

5 Use each **verb** in a sentence. Then change each **verb** to a **noun**. Now use the **noun** in a sentence. Hint! To help you work out the noun, put *the* in front of it.

verb navigate ______________________________

noun __________ ______________________________

verb predict ______________________________

noun __________ ______________________________

verb anticipate ______________________________

noun __________ ______________________________

verb know ______________________________

noun __________ ______________________________

verb develop ______________________________

noun __________ ______________________________

6 Add a **clause** of your own to complete each **sentence**.

Australia's First Nations peoples are called the first astronomers

____

Australia's First Nations peoples used their astrological understanding

____

Being able to anticipate animal movements, ______________________________

____

Predicting when plants were going to be available ______________________________

____

7 *The First Astronomers* is **objective**. Write a **subjective** sentence that gives your opinion about the information provided in the text.

____

____

Research a particular aspect of First Nations peoples' traditional knowledge. You could research how the moon's phases affect fish, or about a particular animal's migration (e.g. the bogong moth) or a useful indigenous plant (e.g. the bunya pine). Present your research to the class.

Unit 15

Clauses, noun groups

This text is the **orientation** for a **science fiction narrative**. It introduces the main **characters** and their problem.

Saving Onega

Once upon a time, on the faraway planet of Onega, there lived two siblings, Ziltox and Zeltar. The siblings were engineers who were working to protect Onega from the Xematars. The Xematars were warrior creatures who lived on Onega's moon. They wanted to colonise Onega for its resources and make the Onegans their slaves but, so far, the Onegans had managed to repel the Xematars.

The Onegan president, President Sulan, had been evacuated to a friendly planet on the far side of Onega, away from Xematar. There, she would be safe from capture while she tried to convince allies in the solar system to support Onega's efforts to stand up to the Xematars.

The Onegans were determined to save their planet, and Ziltox and Zeltar had a plan!

1 Read *Saving Onega*. What problem does Onega face?

___

2 Use a dictionary. Write a definition for each word below used in *Saving Onega*.

engineer ___

colonise ___

repel ___

evacuated ___

allies ___

3 What **predictions** can you make about the rest of the **plot** in the narrative?

___

___

4 Find and underline two **dependent clauses** in *Saving Onega*. Hint! They begin with *who*.

5 Write six **adjectives** of your own to describe the Xematars as you imagine them.

___

6 Join each set of simple sentences to create **complex sentences**.

Jackie has a horse. She loves her horse. It's getting too old to ride on anymore.

____

Helen is a clever girl. She does well in maths. Maths is not her favourite subject.

____

Martin was surprised. His dog wasn't under the house.

____

7 Underline the **nouns** and **noun groups**.

The distant planet with red oceans is known as 'Planet 2315k'.

Jupiter is an uninhabitable giant planet with rings.

Mercury is a rocky planet with a cratered surface.

A massive black hole is devouring stars in a far off galaxy.

Mercury is the fastest planet in our solar system.

Tip

Language can be more or less formal depending on the audience and situation.

Good morning, Principal Bentley, teachers and students. *Hi everyone.*

8 Imagine that President Sulan of Onega is making a **formal** speech to the Onegans. What will she say?

____

____

____

9 Complete the table so that each row provides an interesting scenario for a narrative.

Adjective	Noun	Verb	Adverb
awkward	astronomer	decided	instantly
spine-chilling			
hilarious			
devastating			

Write a **narrative**. Make sure you describe the **characters** and **setting**, and include a problem that the characters have to resolve. Or, complete the rest of the narrative *Saving Onega*. You could create a **storyboard** for your narrative.

Unit 16

Connectives, acronyms, conjunctions

This text discusses the possibility of life on other planets. **Connectives** are used to structure the text.

Does Life Exist on Other Planets?

Is there intelligent life elsewhere in the universe? The SETI Institute was founded to explore this question. SETI stands for Search for Extra-Terrestrial Intelligence.

Some people believe that planet Earth cannot possibly be the only planet in the entire universe to have life. Additionally, scientists believe that other planets could readily have evolved to develop life forms. It seems highly unlikely, however, that these life forms will be similar to those on Earth. The conditions required on another planet would have to exactly match those on Earth for the same patterns of evolution to develop, so it is far more likely that life forms on other planets, if in fact they do exist, are very different from the life forms that have developed on Earth.

Despite the lack of any evidence to support their belief, many people will continue to scan the heavens, fully confident that we are not alone.

Connectives (including conjunctions) link ideas in a text by:

- adding information — *in addition* *as well as*
- providing a reason or cause — *because* *therefore* *so*
- expressing a condition or concession — *although* *if* *unless*
- sequencing information or arguments. — *firstly* *finally* *while*

1 Read *Does Life Exist on Other Planets?* Circle four **connectives**.

2 Why do you think the writer began the text with a **question**?

____

____

3 Use each **connective** in a sentence of your own.

although	unless	therefore	alternatively	likewise

____

____

____

____

____

Grammar Rules! Student Book 5 (ISBN 9780655092537) © Tanya Gibb

4 Circle the **conjunction** in each sentence.

Life developed on Earth so life could have developed elsewhere.

Because scientists are always curious, they will keep searching and wondering.

Life forms might exist on other planets but they are unlikely to look like us.

Although there's no evidence of life elsewhere in the universe, it is still a possibility.

5 The Latin term *terr* means 'earth' or 'land'. Write the definition of *terrestrial.*

____

Write the definition of *extra-terrestrial.*

____

Write five other words based on *terr.*

____

6 What do you think about the possibility of life on other planets? Explain.

____

____

Tip

An **acronym** is made up of the initial letters of other words. SETI stands for **S**earch for **E**xtra-**T**errestrial **I**ntelligence.

7 Use a dictionary to find the meaning of these **acronyms**.

UFO ______________________________

QANTAS ______________________________

NASA ______________________________

radar ______________________________

ANZAC ______________________________

PIN ______________________________

8 Create some **acronyms** for yourself, your friends or family members.

MADO **M**ad **A**nd **D**angerous **O**livia

____

____

Try it yourself!

Design your own planet. Prepare a marketing presentation to 'sell' the idea of moving there to your family. Present the merits of your unique planet and why it would be preferable to live there rather than on Earth.

Unit 17

Statements and questions

This informative text is an **information report**. It presents objective **statements** of fact.

LIFE ON EARTH

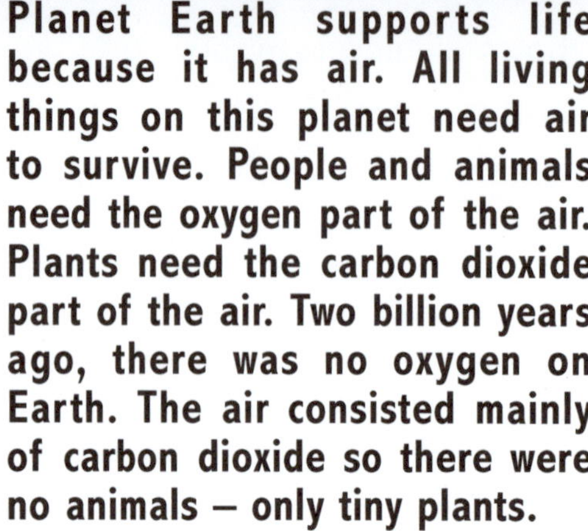

Planet Earth supports life because it has air. All living things on this planet need air to survive. People and animals need the oxygen part of the air. Plants need the carbon dioxide part of the air. Two billion years ago, there was no oxygen on Earth. The air consisted mainly of carbon dioxide so there were no animals – only tiny plants.

Plants use carbon dioxide in a process called photosynthesis. During photosynthesis, plants take in carbon dioxide from the air, and in combination with sunlight, they make energy for their own growth. Oxygen is a by-product of this process. Once oxygen became available on Earth, animals began to evolve.

Earth's air is 21% oxygen. Fires burn oxygen, so any human activity that involves fire uses precious oxygen. If people use up all the oxygen on Earth and there are no plants to regenerate it, animals and people will die.

1 Read *Life on Earth*. Underline all the **verb groups**.
Which two types of **verb** did you find?

1 ______________________ 2 ______________________

What are the two other types of **verbs** that are not used in *Life on Earth*?

1 ______________________ 2 ______________________

Tip Remember the rule on page 11.

Rule

A **statement** gives information or an opinion. It ends in a full stop.
Venus is the second planet from the Sun. *I think Venus looks spectacular.*

A **question** asks for information or an opinion. It ends in a question mark.
What is the time? *Do you think it's time to board the shuttle?*

2 Summarise the facts presented in *Life on Earth*. Write one **statement** for each paragraph.

Paragraph 1 ______________________

Paragraph 2 ______________________

Paragraph 3 ______________________

3 For each paragraph of *Life on Earth*, write one **statement** giving your opinion about the facts.

Paragraph 1 ______________________

Paragraph 2 ______________________

Paragraph 3 ______________________

Grammar Rules! Student Book 5 (ISBN 9780655092537) © Tanya Gibb

Grammar Rules!

_________________________'s Writing Log

1 Plan

What is the purpose of the text?
Who is the audience?
What type of text and text form will you use?
What mode or medium will enhance the presentation?
Gather ideas or research the topic, including using online and digital sources.

2 Draft

Gather and organise your ideas.
Use a graphic organiser or digital tools.
Compose your text.

3 Edit/Revise

Check your work for meaning, clarity and precision.

Is the structure and sequencing appropriate?

Check paragraphing and sentence structures.

Check topic specific vocabulary.

Ask for help to improve your text.

4 Proofread

Check grammar and punctuation.
Check homophones are correct.
Use online dictionaries to check spelling.

5 Publish

Use layout and visual features.
Use digital tools.
Reflect on your work and your text.

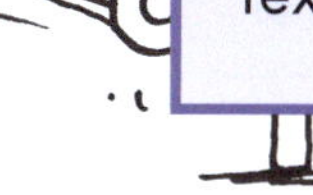

Create symbols for a rating scale. Then each time you finish a piece of writing, record it in the log.

My rating scale

Symbol	Meaning
☐	
☐	
☐	
☐	
☐	

Do you need some ideas for other text forms to try? Look at the back page!

Date	Write the title of your text.	Text purpose and structure	Audienc
Write the date.	Write the title of your piece.	e.g. recount/ email	Who were yo writing for or

Grammar Rules! Student Book 5 (ISBN 9780655092537) © Tanya Gibb

Language features	My rating	Where to next?
ˑ the main grammar and other language tures that you used.	Record your rating.	What grammar could you try next? How could you improve your writing? Does your teacher have any comments?

I've tried these types of texts and text forms . . .

Narrative

- [ ] Story
- [ ] Play script
- [ ] Comic
- [ ] Ballad
- [ ] Retelling a story
- [ ] Poem
- [ ] Song
- [ ] Other ____________________

Recount

- [ ] Letter/email
- [ ] Biography
- [ ] Autobiography
- [ ] News article
- [ ] Imaginative recount
- [ ] Other ____________________

Description

- [ ] Poem
- [ ] Story
- [ ] Play script
- [ ] Biography
- [ ] Advertisement
- [ ] Narrative/story
- [ ] Other ____________________

Informative

- [ ] Information report
- [ ] Website/brochure/leaflet/poster
- [ ] Magazine article
- [ ] Documentary
- [ ] Biography
- [ ] Other ____________________

Procedure

- [ ] Recipe
- [ ] Instructions
- [ ] Rules
- [ ] Directions

Explanation

- [ ] Magazine article
- [ ] Cycle diagram/flow chart
- [ ] Digital chart

Persuasion

- [ ] Debate
- [ ] Argument/speech
- [ ] Letter to editor
- [ ] Editorial
- [ ] TV advertisement
- [ ] Magazine advertisement
- [ ] Radio advertisement
- [ ] Leaflet
- [ ] Music video
- [ ] Blog
- [ ] Poem/song lyrics
- [ ] Other ____________________

Discussion

- [ ] Conversation
- [ ] TV interview
- [ ] Talkback radio
- [ ] Dialogue in a story
- [ ] Panel discussion
- [ ] Formal interview
- [ ] Other ____________________

Response/Reflection

- [ ] Review (film, book, concert, excursion)
- [ ] Diary or journal
- [ ] Poem
- [ ] Other ____________________

4 Write four **questions** that can be answered **objectively** by reading *Life on Earth*.

____

____

____

____

Tip

Questions are sometimes formed by using the structure of a **statement**. In spoken language, a question usually ends in a rising voice.

'You're having dinner with us.' → *'You're having dinner with us?'*

Questions are sometimes formed by adding a **question tag** to the end of a statement or command.

'That's all I have to get.' → *'That's all I have to get, isn't it?'*

5 Write four **statements** based on *Life on Earth* that could be **questions**. Use question marks. Read the questions aloud with a rising inflection. (This means your voice rises at the end of the question.)

____

____

____

____

6 Add a **question tag** to each **statement**.

Shut the door ______________ You are coming ______________

You'll have pizza ______________ You can come ______________

He's coming ______________ We'll be on time ______________

7 Help the alien communicate effectively. It is having trouble with its **relating** and **auxiliary (helping) verbs**. Read this passage aloud, as it is. Then add the correct **verb** forms and read it aloud again.

I _______ from planet Ingula. Ingula _______ 2.2 million megalometres away. Ingula _______ beautiful. Inhabitants of Ingula _______ friendly. Inhabitants _______ happy to _______ friends with Earth people. Earth people _______ good friends. I _______ going back home now. I _______ return soon.

Try it yourself!

Do your own research about the way a particular form of life evolved on Earth. Write an **information report** that includes statements of fact. Use **relating verbs**.

Unit

18 Revision

1 Rewrite the following statements using more **persuasive** language.

Some people think that Toothie Toothpaste works quite well.

You could buy some bananas today, couldn't you?

Do you think you might be able to have a quicker shower?

2 Number the sentences from 1 to 4. 1 is for least forceful or certain and 4 is for most forceful or certain.

- ☐ Prepare for take-off.
- ☐ Would you mind preparing for take-off?
- ☐ You should prepare for take-off.
- ☐ It's probably time for you to prepare for take-off.

3 Underline the **thinking verb** in each row.

believe	jump	gobble	carrot
broccoli	hope	jelly	devoured
wonder	rainbow	destroy	comet
chance	solar	proceed	enjoy

4 Write a **complex sentence**. Make sure it has three or more **clauses**.

5 Rewrite each sentence with correct punctuation.

mum gave me a chemistry set for my birthday said lennie

do you know the poem Jabberwocky asked ryan

astronauts need to be intelligent motivated resilient adaptable and physically fit said leisl

Grammar Rules! Student Book 5 (ISBN 9780655092537) © Tanya Gibb

6 Use each **verb** in a sentence. Then change each **verb** to a **noun**. Now use the **noun** in a sentence.

verb arresting ______________________________

noun ____________ ______________________________

verb growing ______________________________

noun ____________ ______________________________

verb dying ______________________________

noun ____________ ______________________________

verb leaping ______________________________

noun ____________ ______________________________

7 Write the **singular forms** of these nouns.

millennia ____________ media ____________ foci ____________ fungi ____________

cact ____________ octopi ____________ hippopotami ____________ axes ____________

crises ____________ bacteria ____________ indices ____________ appendices ____________

8 Use each **connective** in a text of your own to link ideas.

firstly	alternatively	therefore	even though

____

____

____

____

9 Rewrite each **sentence** so that events have already occurred.

We might have pizzas for dinner tonight.

____

Lulu and Simon will visit in the morning.

____

10 Write the words that each **acronym** stands for. Use a dictionary if necessary.

RAM ______________________________ laser ______________________________

Unit 19

Synonyms, paragraphs, sentences, features of voice

This text **advocates** for community action on a local area preservation issue. It is a **formal persuasive** speech.

Save Our Wetlands

Good afternoon, everyone and welcome.

I begin by acknowledging the Traditional Custodians of the lands on which we meet, and pay respect to their Elders, past and present.

Thank you for attending today. We have gathered to discuss the proposed resort development on our precious coastal wetlands. We understand that some Council members support the construction of the resort on the wetlands site because they say the development will benefit our community. I am here to refute that claim and urge you to protect the wetlands.

The wetlands are vital to us all for many reasons, but they are especially vital to the survival of migratory birds such as bar-tailed godwits. Godwits travel halfway around the globe, from Alaska to these wetlands, nonstop every year. They and other animals depend on these wetlands for survival.

Let's put nature ahead of profits. Will you join me in saving the wetlands for migratory birds and the other plants and animals that depend on them?

1 Read *Save Our Wetlands*. What is the **main idea** in the text?

____

2 Write six **synonyms** for *wetlands*. Hint! Synonyms are words with similar meanings.

____

3 Find **synonyms** in the text for the following words.

contradict __________	treasured __________	persuade __________
help __________	rely __________	wealth __________
location __________	essential __________	protect __________

4 Explain the purpose of each **paragraph** in the text after the greeting.

Paragraph 1 ________________________________

Paragraph 2 ________________________________

Paragraph 3 ________________________________

Paragraph 4 ________________________________

Grammar Rules! Student Book 5 (ISBN 9780655092537) © Tanya Gibb

5 Write the **verb** forms to show **past tense**.

Base form	Past tense	Past tense with auxiliary
advocate	I	I
migrate	They	They
acknowledge	I	I
attend	I	I
construct	I	I
understand	I	I

6 Draw a line to correctly link each **noun group** with the rest of the sentence.

Various wetlands	is a treaty between nations to promote the conservation of wetlands.
The bar-tailed godwit	is the greatest threat to migratory birds.
Habitat loss	can be guided by western science as well as Traditional Owners' knowledge.
Many migratory birds	has a vital role.
The Ramsar Convention	hold significant cultural value for Australia's First Peoples.
Invasive species	are protected by international agreements.
Land management practices	threaten biodiversity of wetlands.
Every component of an ecosystem	links wetlands on two continents.

The **volume**, **pitch**, **pace** and **tone** of your voice can be used for effect when making spoken presentations.

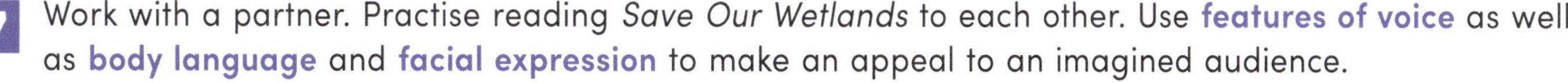

7 Work with a partner. Practise reading *Save Our Wetlands* to each other. Use **features of voice** as well as **body language** and **facial expression** to make an appeal to an imagined audience.

Do some research and list five extra reasons to support protecting wetlands. Create a *Save Our Wetlands* poster. Or, choose a local issue and create a campaign poster, petition or video to advocate for what you want to happen.

Unit 20 Evaluative language

War of the Worlds

Most film critics agree that *War of the Worlds*, released in 2005, is one of the best science fiction movies of all time. Film critics have consistently and overwhelmingly been positive about the film, agreeing that it is exciting and suspenseful and that the special effects are seamless.

The film's plot is credible because it is possible to believe that creatures from outer space could attempt to conquer Earth with superior technology and weaponry but be defeated by microscopic organisms, such as bacteria or viruses for which they have no natural biological defenses.

This film is rated M and is highly recommended for families with children over 12 years of age. It has a positive message about looking after family members, too.

Tip Reviews include **judgements** or **evaluations**. Reviews can be more influential if they refer to authoritative sources rather that simply present the writer/speaker's opinion.
I think the movie is... → *Most scientists agree that...*

1 Read *War of the Worlds*. Underline references to **authoritative sources** in the review.

2 Read *War of the Worlds*. Tick a column for each of these **statements**.

Statement	Fact/Objective	Evaluation/ Subjective
War of the Worlds was released in 2005.		
The special effects were really clever.		
It was exciting and scary.		
The story was actually quite believable.		
I highly recommend this movie.		
I loved it!		
War of the Worlds is a movie.		

3 Write six **adjectives** used in *War of the Worlds*.

Grammar Rules! Student Book 5 (ISBN 9780655092537) © Tanya Gibb

4 Imagine you saw *War of the Worlds* and you hated it. Write the opposite **evaluations** to the ones below. Write with certainty.

Evaluation	Opposite evaluation
The plot was extremely clever.	______________________
The acting was really terrible.	______________________
The characters were not believable.	______________________
Everyone will really enjoy this movie.	______________________
It is the best science fiction movie of all time.	______________________

5 Circle the **adverb** in each row.

long	longingly	lengthy	lateral
lovingly	love	loving	loveless
luscious	lush	tropical	typically
great	fantastic	hopeless	hopelessly

6 Circle the **adverbs** that tell manner (how) in *War of the Worlds*.

7 Write five **adjectives** you could use to describe a film you did not enjoy.

____

____

8 Circle the statement in each pair that you think would be more influential.

I think it's a great film.	Critics agree that it's a great film.
Many people were impressed with the book.	People have generally been impressed with the book.
Audiences the world over love the story.	I absolutely love the story.
Most reviewers were disappointed with the ending.	I thought the ending was VERY disappointing.

Exclamation marks are used to emphasise words that are said loudly or in surprise, anger, fear or happiness.

Wow! *Get away from there!* *Yummy!*

9 Imagine you are watching a very scary science fiction movie. Write three **exclamations** that you might make.

____

____

____

Write a review of a movie that you like or dislike. Include **evaluative language** (**adjectives** and **adverbs**) and use **authoritative sources** to support your claims. Avoid using the pronoun 'I'.

Unit 21

Commas, dependent clauses

The Sky Emu

Australia's First Nations peoples have traditional stories that explain or describe celestial phenomena and the relationships between Earth and the universe. These stories have been passed on from one generation to the next over millennia.

A sky emu features in many First Nations stories. The Wiradjuri people of central New South Wales call the sky emu 'Gugurmin'. You can see Gugurmin's head, neck, body and legs in the dark patches of the Milky Way.

During the year, as the Earth travels around the sun, the emu is in different positions in the night sky. Its position tells the Wiradjuri people important information, such as the time of year for traditional ceremonies, when to expect waterholes to be full and when emu eggs will be available.

Between December and February, Gugurmin is below the horizon and cannot be seen. On Wiradjuri country, when you can't see Gugurmin, it means the waterholes will all be dry.

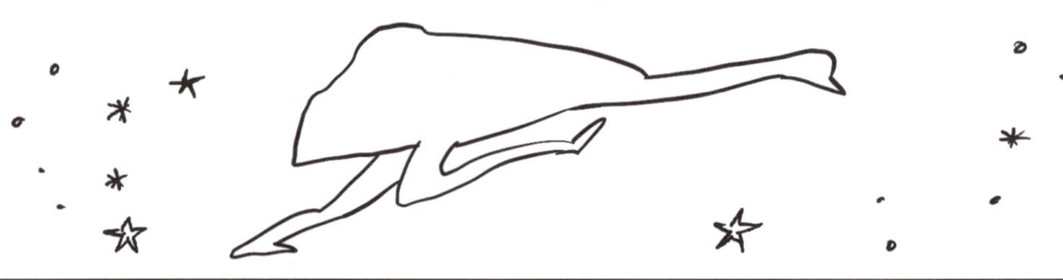

This informative text **explains** a natural phenomenon and its meaning to Australia's First Nations peoples.

Rule

Commas separate items in a list and phrases in a sentence, as well as

- a dependent clause from a main clause when the dependent clause comes first in the sentence
  While Jack was out, the mischievous little alien ransacked his home.
- quoted speech in a sentence. *'I'll be back in an hour,' said Ely.*

1 Read *The Sky Emu*. Copy the sentence that uses **commas** to separate items in a list.

____

2 What is the function of the comma in this sentence?

When you can't see Gugurmin from Wiradjuri country, it means the waterholes will all be dry.

____

3 Write definitions for the words below.

celestial ________________________________

phenomena ________________________________

Grammar Rules! Student Book 5 (ISBN 9780655092537) © Tanya Gibb

4 Write **objective** or **subjective** after each statement.

> **Tip** Remember the rule on page 27.

The International Space Station (ISS) is a joint project of the USA, Japan, Russia, Canada and Europe. ________________

More countries should contribute funding for the ISS. ________________

The ISS should be dismantled because it's too costly. ________________

Space Station MIR orbited the earth from 1986 until 2001. ________________

Altogether, MIR travelled over three and half billion kilometres. ________________

Australian astronaut Andy Thomas' first space flight was on the *Endeavour*. ________________

MIR was the world's first long-term space research station. ________________

> **Tip** Words for people can sometimes be formed by changing the **suffix** or ending on a noun or a verb. *Astronomy* → *astronaut*
> (Note: The prefix *astro* means 'planets, stars, space'. *Naut* is from an Ancient Greek word meaning 'sailor'. So, an *astronaut* is 'a sailor in space'.)

5 Change the ending of each noun to name a person. Use a dictionary.

Paediatrics → *paediatrician*

city ________________

refuge ________________

inhabit ________________

journal ________________

science ________________

advise ________________

piano ________________

surgery ________________

6 Add **commas** where they belong in the sentences below. Circle the **independent clauses**.

When you visit Mount Borradaile you can see rock art that is at least 55,000 years old.

At Windjana Gorge rock art depicts the Wandjina ancestral creation being.

Since ancient times people have been fascinated by the night sky.

While observing the stars people created stories to make sense of their world.

Find a text written by a First Nations author that explains how a natural phenomenon is understood in their culture. Create your own written, spoken or visual text to explain the phenomenon to others in your class.

Unit

22

Noun groups, prepositional phrases, figurative language

This poem uses **technical terms** and **prepositional phrases** to describe places in the environment.

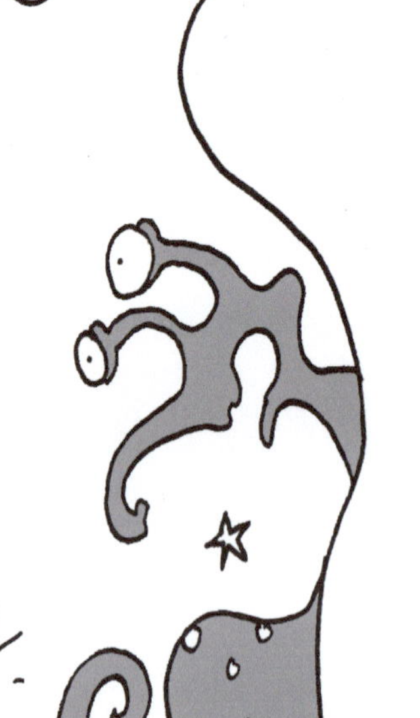

OUR EARTH

One biosphere
encompassing
all life:
microorangisms,
plants,
animals.
From the highest mountains
to the deepest trenches
in the ocean;
from sandy deserts
to green grasslands;
from lush rainforests
to the frozen tundra;
everywhere –
there is life.
One biosphere
sustaining life:
a bubble.

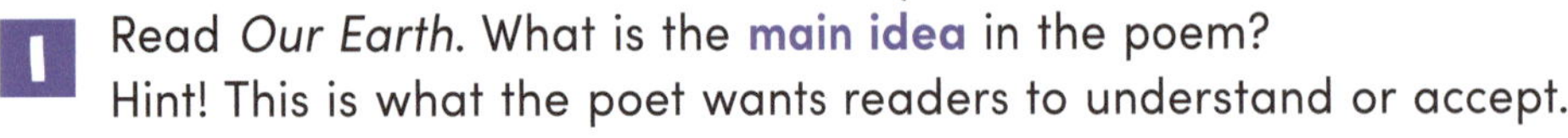

1 Read *Our Earth*. What is the **main idea** in the poem?
Hint! This is what the poet wants readers to understand or accept.

____

____

2 Copy the three compound words used in *Our Earth*.

____

3 Underline the **noun groups** in *Our Earth*.

4 Circle the **prepositional phrases** in *Our Earth*. Hint! A prepositional phrase consists of a preposition and a noun group or pronoun.

5 Write the **verbs** used in *Our Earth*. ____

6 The Greek words *bios* means 'life' and *sphaira* means 'sphere'. Use a dictionary to find and list other words in English that come from these Greek words.

bio ____

sphere ____

Grammar Rules! Student Book 5 (ISBN 9780655092537) © Tanya Gibb

Figurative language provides ways of looking at the world imaginatively. It includes **metaphor**, where one thing is said to be another (*the snow is a blanket*), and **simile**, where things are compared using 'like' or 'as' (*He runs like the wind. She is as fast as the wind.*).

7 What is the **metaphor** in *Our Earth*?

____

8 Read the text below.

Traditional stories of the Kaurna people of South Australia say the Milky Way is a river in the sky world. Camp fires burn along the river, twinkling like stars. Dark patches in the river are called Yurakauwe. Yurakauwe means monster water. A dangerous monster called Yura lives there.

What is the **metaphor**? ______________________________

What is the **simile**? ______________________________

9 Read the text below.

Hungarian mythology says the Milky Way is 'The Road of the Warriors.' The Hungarian ancestor character Csaba rides down the Milky Way to save the people. The sparks from the horse's shoes are the stars.

Create a **metaphor** for the text.

____

Create a **simile** for the text.

____

10 Read the text below. Circle the **connectives**.

A traditional tale of the Cherokee people of North America says that the Milky Way was created when a dog stole some cornmeal and as the people chased it away, it spilt the cornmeal across the sky, creating the Milky Way. The Cherokee name for the Milky Way means 'where the dog ran'.

11 List evidence from the texts in questions 8, 9 and 10 that reflect culture, place and time.

____

____

____

____

Have you ever viewed something in wonder? It might be something in nature or an animal. Write a poem to describe it and your feelings about it. Use **figurative language** so that readers can develop a mental picture.

Unit 23

Greek and Latin word roots, clauses, sentences

This text is **informative** and **objective**. It uses technical terminology.

Ecological Footprint

Every human being uses resources, such as food and energy and creates waste, such as pollution. This impact on the environment, which each person makes, can be called an 'ecological footprint'. Each person's footprint can be measured, and each community, organisation, workplace and country can also have its ecological footprint measured.

Ecological footprints are measured by calculating goods and services used, and the energy and resources required to create them, as well as the waste products left over and the ways the waste is dealt with, stored or eliminated.

Conservation groups have predicted that to continue with current global consumption and pollution levels, we'll need the resources of 12 planet Earths.

1 Read *Ecological Footprint.* Use a dictionary to find a definition for each of these **technical terms** in the text.

resources ______________________________

pollution ______________________________

ecological ______________________________

eliminated ______________________________

conservation ______________________________

consumption ______________________________

Many words in English are from Latin or Greek words. Recognising word origins and roots helps you read new words, work out word meanings and spell unknown words.
Chronos is the Greek god of time. *Chronology* means events in time order.

2 Find examples for each **word base**. Write them in the column.

Word Base	Meaning	Examples
bronch- (Latin)	windpipe	
cent- (Latin)	hundred	
cycl- (Greek)	circular	
dur- (Latin)	hard	
dem- (Greek)	people	
pan- (Greek)	all	
ped- (Latin)	foot	
zo- (Greek)	animal	

3 Rewrite each pair of sentences as a **complex sentence**. Use **commas** and a **pronoun** from the box.

who	who	whose	which

The impact on the environment can be called an 'ecological footprint'. Each person makes one.

The impact on the environment, which each person makes, can be called an 'ecological footprint'.

My mother works for the government. She is an accountant.

____

The house is 100 years old. It is owned by the Historical Trust.

____

Sarah's home was damaged in the flood. Sarah now lives with her grandma.

____

My sister is on the football team. She trains hard.

____

4 Rewrite each pair of sentences as a single sentence. Use a **conjunction** from the box.

so	and	neither/nor	either/or	because

One person can come. It can be Bobby or Bernie. Either Bobby or Bernie can come.

The car had a flat tyre. Jane was late for school.

____

Bill has a new pencil case. Jenny has a new pencil case.

____

Someone will help you calculate your ecological footprint. It will be Chen or Hamish.

____

Jana hasn't got a new pencil case. Jim hasn't got a new pencil case.

____

We don't have 12 planet Earths. We need to make sure that whatever resources we use, we can renew or reuse, and whatever waste products we create, we can dispose of safely.

____

____

Use the internet to work out your own ecological footprint or that of your home or school. Create an **information report**. Add images and create a multimodal presentation to present the information to the class.

Unit 24 Revision

1 Write a **simple sentence** that begins with a **verb** or **verb group**.

____

2 Rewrite this sentence in the **past tense**.

I will go to visit my sick uncle in hospital.

____

3 Complete the table.

Base form	Past tense	Past tense with auxiliary
study	I	I
understand	I	I
dream	I	I
teach	I	I
think	I	I

4 Write whether each **statement** is **objective** or **subjective**.

Dogs are mammals. ____________

Dogs are cute. ____________

The book I'm reading is really funny. ____________

My mum cooks great stir-fry. ____________

My tree house has a launch pad. ____________

5 Write the opposite **evaluation**. Write with the same degree of certainty.

Evaluation	Opposite evaluation
My dog will win.	______________________
My new bicycle was poorly made.	______________________
I love summer the best.	______________________
My dad is a spectacular dancer.	______________________

6 Add an **adjective** and an **adverb** that tells manner (how) to each sentence.

The ______________ gymnast tumbled ______________.

A ______________ man fell ______________.

The ______________ baby cried ______________.

The ______________ child grumbled ______________.

7 Rewrite each group of sentences as a single **complex sentence**. Use words from the box.

who that which so and

It was cold. I wore my overcoat. My mum had bought me the overcoat.

It was cold so I wore the overcoat that my mum had bought me.

It was hot. We went for a swim in the neighbour's pool. The neighbours had just built a pool.

____

My mum bought me a bike. My mum bought me a helmet. I had always wanted a bike and helmet.

____

My friend lives across the road. My friend has a dog that bites.

____

8 Rewrite the **sentences**. Use correct **punctuation**.

sashas telescope allows him to see saturn from his backyard

____

when rae visited mount borradaile she saw 55,000 year old rock art

____

translated from latin astronaut means a sailor in space

____

9 Use each **pronoun** in a **complex sentence**.

who	______________________________
whose	______________________________
which	______________________________

10 Use each **conjunction** in a **complex sentence**.

neither/nor either/or because

____

____

____

____

____

11 Write a **simile** to describe a bright, sunny day.

____

Unit 25

Emotive language, reported (indirect) speech, inclusive language

Daily Chronicle, 1 April 2046

MASS PANIC – UFO TERRORISES CITY

Naarm came to a sudden standstill today as people abandoned cars and workplaces, terrified, as a UFO, the size of three football fields, ominously hovered above the city.

As yet, officials have been unable to communicate with the saucer. Police, emergency services and defence personnel are liaising to coordinate their strategies and any response to an attack by the UFO on the city.

Speculation, at this stage, suggests the saucer is a solitary vessel. Police Commissioner Gowri Neal has confirmed that no other spaceships have been sighted.

Police are urging all citizens to stay inside their homes and not panic. They are also advising sightseers to remain clear of the area until it can be determined whether or not the UFO is a threat.

1 Read *Mass Panic – UFO Terrorises City*. Write five **emotive** words it uses that sensationalise the topic. Then suggest a non-sensational **synonym** for each one. Hint! Synonyms are words that are similar in meaning.

monstrous → big ______________________

______________________ ______________________

______________________ ______________________

2 Write the **adverb** that tells how the UFO hovered. What does it mean?

____

Rule **Reported (indirect) speech** is speech that is not quoted directly. It does not need quotation marks.

Police Commissioner Gowri Neal has confirmed that the aliens have taken over.

3 Why does the newspaper include Police Commissioner Gowri Neal's **reported speech**?

____

____

4 Add to the newspaper article. Include the **reported speech** of a military commander to give the military's perspective on the UFO.

____

____

____

Grammar Rules! Student Book 5 (ISBN 9780655092537) © Tanya Gibb

5 Rewrite the **quoted speech** as **reported speech**.

'The UFO is terrifying!' cried a Melbourne worker.

'We've been unable to communicate,' said Police Commissioner Gowri Neal.

'I'm so excited,' said one witness. 'I'm taking lots of photos!'

'I think it's a solitary vessel,' suggested one reporter.

'Stay clear of the area,' the police officer warned the public.

Use **gender inclusive** language when you don't want to exclude one gender or show bias.

gender exclusive *Mankind is creating climate change.*

gender inclusive *People are creating climate change.*

6 Rewrite each sentence using **gender inclusive** language.

Mankind can no longer afford to be complacent about the environment.

Every student is required to bring her own lunch on the excursion.

When any president visits the city, he stays at the conference venue.

Cavemen developed simple tools to assist him in his daily life.

Phone all the schools and ask each principal if he can attend our meeting.

7 Consider the **headline** *Mass Panic – UFO Terrorises City*. Would the headline attract readers' attention? Does the headline match what is covered in the article? Explain.

Write a news report about a UFO landing in your community. Use **emotive language** to sensationalise the report. Include the **quoted** or **reported** speech of witnesses.

Unit 26

Adjectives, adjectival phrases, verbs

This informative text provides a **description**. It uses **adjectives** and **adjectival phrases** to accurately describe the subject.

MARS, THE RED PLANET

Mars is the fourth planet from the sun. It is very, very cold, with temperatures ranging from –123 °C to 17 °C. Mars has north and south poles with frozen ice caps like Earth. Mars has two moons.

The surface of Mars is cratered and strewn with rocks. Mars is called the red planet because it is rich in iron, which rusts, making the soil and dust red. Mars has very strong winds of up to 200 kilometres per hour and severe red dust storms that can engulf the whole planet for months on end.

Mars has the tallest volcano in our solar system. It is called Olympus Mons. Mars also has some of the deepest valleys in our solar system. At certain times of the year, it is possible to see Mars from Earth with the naked eye.

1 Read *Mars, the Red Planet*. Create an interesting **noun group** for each main **noun**. Do not use **adjectives** already used in *Mars, the Red Planet*.

mountain	dust storms	surface	planet

____

____

____

____

2 Turn these **nouns** into **adjectives**. Then use each **adjective** in a sentence.
mischief→ mischievous. The mischievous child caused chaos in the classroom.

hero ______________ ______________________________

colour ______________ ______________________________

trouble ______________ ______________________________

disaster ______________ ______________________________

3 Use a **relating verb** or **verb group** to complete each sentence.

has been	are	belong	will become

Mars and Earth ______________ planets in our solar system.

Two moons ______________ to Mars.

Mars ______________ the subject of many books and movies over the years.

Mars ______________ a destination for astronauts of the future.

Tip Remember the rule on page 22.

4 Read *Mars, the Red Planet*. Circle a **complex sentence**.

Grammar Rules! Student Book 5 (ISBN 9780655092537) © Tanya Gibb

5 Here are some **verbs** to represent the way a Martian might eat.
Create a **noun group** for a food item for each one.

Doing verb	Noun group
crunched	two crispy, brittle crater cookies
slobbered	
swallowed	
chewed	
gnawed	

Adjectival phrases do the job of an **adjective**. They describe a **noun**.
Adjectival phrases often go after the **noun** they modify.

The Martian <u>with hairy ears</u> is my teacher.

6 Circle the **adjectival phrases**.

The dog with the loud bark lives next door.

The player in spiked shoes is disqualified.

The plant with the dead leaves gets too much sun.

Any child without a hat must stay indoors.

The bike with the big motor is Grandma's.

Comparative and **superlative adjectives** show degrees of comparison. **Adjectives** with more than two syllables usually use *more* for **comparative** and *most* for **superlative**.

	positive	**comparative**	**superlative**
regular	*happy*	*happier*	*happiest*
irregular	*good*	*better*	*best*
more syllables	*beautiful*	*more beautiful*	*most beautiful*

7 Complete the table.

Positive	Comparative	Superlative
dusty		
empty		
remote		
unusual		

Write a **descriptive** travel brochure about Mars. Use interesting **noun groups** that will encourage travellers to visit. Let travellers know what they will see, hear, touch, feel, wonder at and experience.

Unit 27

Prepositional phrases, tense

How is the Earth Magnetic?

The centre of the Earth is a solid core that is mostly made of iron. Around the solid core is a liquid layer of molten iron.

As the Earth rotates, it causes movement in this molten iron layer. This in turn creates electric currents. These currents generate a magnetic field giving planet Earth the properties of a magnet.

Earth's magnetic field reaches out thousands of kilometres into space. However, the Earth's magnetism is too weak to cause metal objects to fly through the air as the Earth rotates. Imagine what would happen if Earth's magnetism were stronger!

This informative text is an **explanation**. It includes a sequence of events linked through cause and effect.

1 Read *How is the Earth Magnetic?* Use a dictionary and write the definitions for the **technical terms** used.

magnet ______________________________

magnetic field ______________________________

iron ______________________________

molten iron ______________________________

electric current ______________________________

rotates ______________________________

2 Underline the **prepositional phrases** used in *How is the Earth Magnetic?*

3 Underline the **prepositional phrases** that tell manner (how). Circle the **prepositional phrases** that tell place (where).

Tip: Remember the rule on page 20.

Planet Earth could be said to have a magnet at its centre.

Around the solid core is liquid iron.

Magnetic fields are caused by electric currents.

They travelled on foot across the rocky terrain.

It would be unpleasant to be hit on the head with an iron.

An iron pan flying through the air would cause damage.

4 Use each **prepositional phrase** that tells time (when) in a sentence.

during the flight	since the beginning	until Monday
for a long time	before the cyclone	

____

____

____

____

____

5 Complete each label on the diagram with one of these **prepositional phrases**. Hint! You'll find the information in *How is the Earth Magnetic?*

by Earth's rotation	for thousands of kilometres	at its centre

Planet Earth has a lot of iron ______________________.

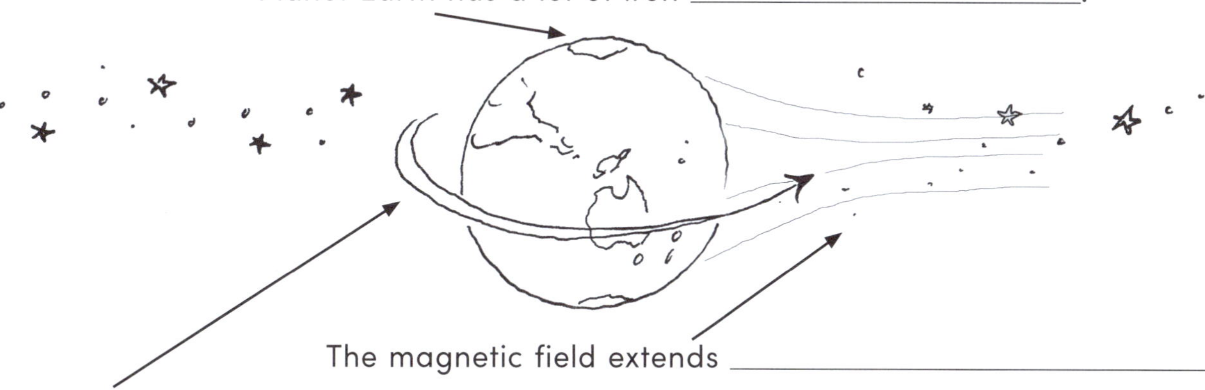

The magnetic field extends ___________________________.

Electric currents are generated _________________________.

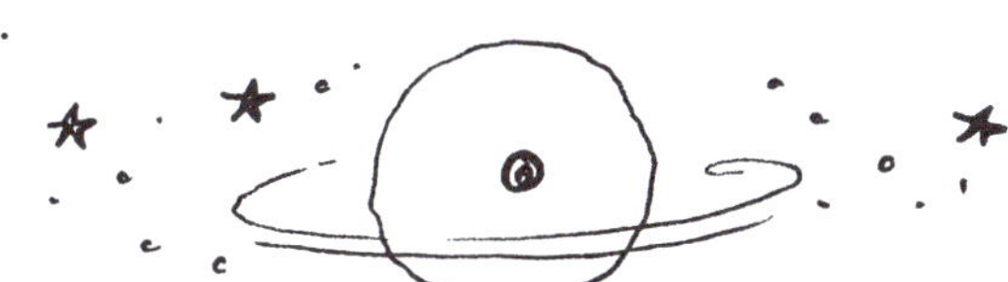

6 Rewrite each **present tense** sentence in the **past tense**.

The centre of the Earth is solid and mostly made of iron.

____

Around the solid core is a liquid layer of molten iron.

____

The electric currents generate a magnetic field.

____

Earth has the properties of a magnet.

____

Now read your **past tense** sentences. Does past tense make sense in this explanation? Why or why not?

____

____

____

Explanations are often accompanied by diagrams or flow charts. Do some research on a topic of your choice. Write an **explanation**. Draw a diagram or flow chart to illustrate the concepts in your explanation.

Unit 28 Text connectives, addressing an audience

The writer of this letter to the editor of a newspaper argues a **point of view**. Ideas are linked using **connectives**. The writer uses **emotive** and **forceful language** to convince readers to agree with their point of view.

Who Needs Science?

Dear Editor,

In response to N. Baines (20th Sept.) who said that 'schools absolutely must ditch science in favour of students spending more time on literacy and numeracy activities': firstly, I wish to remind N. Baines that without science, life would definitely be much less interesting. Readers, think of any appliance or product in your home. Science is involved.

Secondly, N. Baines obviously doesn't realise that science enables us to understand our world and its phenomena. Without this understanding and the human capacity to explore, experiment and wonder, we could well have remained living in caves. Science improves and enriches our lives.

Lastly, modern science in the classroom includes an ethical component that teaches students to be responsible decision-makers and consider the ethics of all their actions.

I'm happy to have science in my life. Go back to your cave, N. Baines.

Yours sincerely,

Proud Scientist

1 Read *Who Needs Science?* Circle the **connectives** that link the arguments.

Remember the rule on page 38.

2 What is implied by the **command** 'Go back to your cave?'

3 Rewrite the following sentences more forcefully or with greater certainty.

School children probably need more exercise, so we might have sport and games more often.

Maybe school children could have excursions to chocolate factories.

4 Rewrite these statements less forcefully or with less certainty.

Brussels sprouts absolutely improve and enrich our lives.

Schools should definitely have stargazing sleep-outs in their playgrounds every term.

Sometimes, during a discussion, it is better to express opinions less forcefully to allow for negotiation and compromise.

5 Pretend you are Proud Scientist and you are speaking to N. Baines in person. Finish each sentence. Be polite and non-argumentative.

I wonder, have you considered ______________________________

____

Have you thought about ______________________________

____

Possibly you haven't realised that ______________________________

____

6 Write the slang word in *Who Needs Science?* that means 'to get rid of'.

____

Audiences are addressed differently depending on their relationship with the speaker or writer.

informal, friendly: *Johnno, pass me the bag.*

formal, respectful: *Excuse me, sir, could you please pass me the bag?*

7 Underline the terms used to address the **audience** in each greeting.

Please, madam, explain how science improves our lives.

May I have your attention, ladies and gentlemen?

Don't you think, dear reader, that science is important?

Colleagues, thank you for meeting with me.

Hey, honey, do you think that scientist is a mad scientist?

8 Why might N. Baines want to replace science in favour of literacy and numeracy? Write some possible reasons.

____

____

9 Write a sentence as yourself to address Proud Scientist.

____

Write a letter to an editor about an issue that concerns you. Write three main arguments and link them using **connectives** such as *firstly, secondly, finally*. Express your ideas with certainty to convince readers to adopt your point of view.

Unit 29

Emotive language, subjective language

This **persuasive text** is the opening argument in a **formal** parliamentary-style debate. It uses **emotive** and **subjective language** to engage the audience.

Animal Experimentation is Wrong

Speaker 1: Good afternoon, everyone. Today, my team and I will argue most convincingly that using animals for scientific experimentation is cruel, immoral and absolutely unnecessary.

My first example of animal abuse is the space program. Animals such as apes, mice, spiders, dogs, cats, bats, beetles, tortoises and guinea pigs have been used in space programs since the 1940s. Many, many of these animals died in space. Many died on re-entry or landing and many landed safely but were murdered by scientists for information that might be gained from autopsies. The four monkeys all known only as Albert – I, II, III and IV – all died horrible deaths in the name of science. A US Navy-trained squirrel monkey, named Gordo, drowned when he crashed into the sea and sank in his landing module nose cone. Now, I ask you, intelligent audience, what possible benefit to human space flight can result from sending tortoises and guinea pigs into space?

Tip Using **emotive** language to appeal to people's emotions can sometimes help to win an argument. At other times, it is better to be objective.

1 Read *Animal Experimentation is Wrong*. Write four **emotive words** or **phrases** used.

____

2 How does the creator of the text *Animal Experimentation is Wrong* want you to feel about the topic?

____

3 What **claims** would a speaker need to make to argue that animal experimentation is NOT wrong?

____

____

4 What advantage does the speaker hope to gain by including the squirrel monkey's name, Gordo, in the debate? ______________________________

____

5 Circle five **verb groups** in *Animal Experimentation is Wrong* that include **auxiliary verbs**.

6 Underline a **complex sentence** in *Animal Experimentation is Wrong*.

Grammar Rules! Student Book 5 (ISBN 9780655092537) © Tanya Gibb

7 Circle the **noun groups** in the complex sentence below.

A U.S. Navy-trained squirrel monkey, named Gordo, drowned when his landing module nose cone crashed into the sea and sank.

Tip Remember the rule on page 27.

8 Write **subjective** or **objective** after each statement.

Polio is a devastating disease with no cure. ________________

Polio is a highly contagious disease that affects the spinal cord, potentially causing paralysis. ________________

Animal experimentation to find a cure for polio began in the 1930s on monkeys, mice, guinea pigs and rabbits. ________________

Dr Jonas Salk developed a polio vaccine and, incredibly, trialled it on himself and his family in 1953. ________________

Albert Sabin developed a different kind of vaccine from Salk's and trialled it on himself and his family. ________________

Salk's vaccine is swallowed and is therefore easy to administer. ________________

9 Mark the scale to show the relationship between speaker and listener that is implied by each form of address. 1 is the closest relationship and 5 is the most distant relationship.

	closest				most distant
Where are you, Mum?	1	2	3	4	5
I'm pleased to introduce Ms Yuki...	1	2	3	4	5
Good morning, viewers.	1	2	3	4	5
Hey, Bubby.	1	2	3	4	5
Welcome, Science Club...	1	2	3	4	5

10 Add a clause to complete each sentence below to express opinions about any topic you choose.

Experts have stated that ____.

It could be said that ____.

It is generally agreed that ____.

Many people expect that ____.

Write a **speech** to respond to the first speaker of the *Animal Experimentation is Wrong* debate. Or, do some research and write the second speaker's argument in support of the statement that *Animal Experimentation is Wrong*. Appeal directly to your **audience**.

Unit 30 Revision

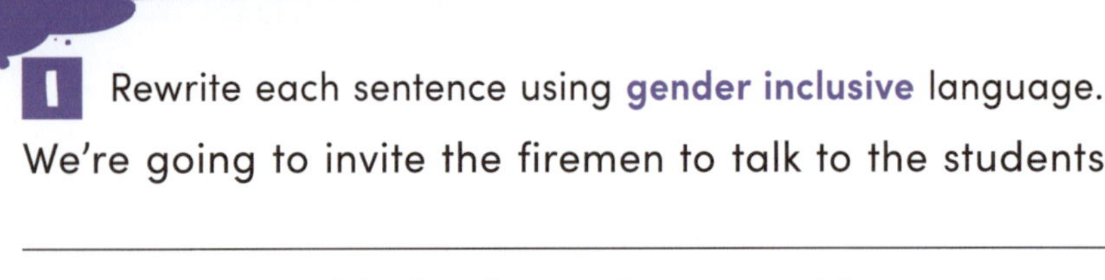

1 Rewrite each sentence using **gender inclusive** language.

We're going to invite the firemen to talk to the students.

____

Man is responsible for the environmental issues.

____

I'll find a doctor and have him call you.

____

2 Rewrite the **quoted speech** as **reported speech**.

'Olympus Mons is named after Mount Olympus, the home of the Greek gods,' announced Karli.

____

'Did you know that the Romans named Mars after their god of war because of its red colour?' asked Sebastien. ____

____

3 Underline the **prepositional phrases** that tell manner (how). Circle the **prepositional phrases** that tell place (where).

I went to see a movie at the cinema.

Tie a ribbon around the tree.

The howling sound is caused by the wind.

Hamish looked with sad eyes at his empty bowl.

4 Create an interesting **noun group** for each main **noun**.

tree	______________________
sky	______________________
earthquake	______________________
thunderstorm	______________________
soil	______________________

5 Use a **relating verb** to complete each sentence.

The koala ________________ a marsupial.

Dogs ________________ an excellent sense of smell.

We ________________ happy with our last holiday.

Praveen and Carolyn ________________ in Sydney.

A tadpole ________________ a frog.

6 Change these **nouns** to **adjectives**. Then use each **adjective** in a sentence.

wind ______________ ____

scene ______________ ____

danger ______________ ____

7 Underline the **adjectival phrases**.

The beach towel with the yellow stripes is Kara's.

The dancer in the leather jacket is my favourite.

The painting of the actor is for sale.

The speech by the principal was very moving.

Children with hats can go outside.

8 Complete the table.

Positive	Comparative	Superlative
dirty		
spacious		
busy		
hungry		

9 Sensationalise each sentence by rewriting it using **emotive** language.

Vandals caused a lot of damage.

____

The rain caused flooding overnight near Maitland.

____

10 Mark the scale to show the relationship between speaker and listener that is implied by each greeting. 1 is the closest relationship and 5 is the most distant relationship.

	closest				most distant
Hi, Josh!	1	2	3	4	5
How can I help you, madam?	1	2	3	4	5
Good morning, students.	1	2	3	4	5
Ladies and gentlemen...	1	2	3	4	5

11 Link the arguments by writing each **connective** on the correct line.

finally
firstly
in addition

I prefer to watch films at the cinema instead of at home on DVD. ______________, I like to see a movie as soon as possible – I don't want to have to wait until it is available for home viewing. ______________, I think it's more exciting to see a movie on a big cinema screen. ______________, I like to get out, not stay at home every night.

Unit 31

Idiom, simile, metaphor, informal language, verb groups

This text is a written communication to the writer's friend. It gives the writer's point of view and uses **idiomatic**, **informal language** as well as **simile** and **metaphor**.

New Message

Hi Nicco,

I am so annoyed. I really, really wanted to go camping with Tash's family BUT my restrictive, prohibitive, unreasonable parents, the jail-keepers, would not allow it. It's like a prison here. I look out the window and I can't see any stars.

Once in a blue moon I ask for something. If I could have gone camping, I would have been able to see soooooo many constellations.

Tash found a website that tells you how to measure with hand spans and finger widths and where to find all the interesting objects in the night sky in the Southern Hemisphere. It's a really cool site.

I'd have been over the moon to go camping. I should have been allowed. Grrrr!

1 Complete the sentences using prepositional phrases from *New Message*.

Tip: Remember the rule on page 20.

When the writer looks ______________________________,
they can't see any stars.

Tash found a website that tells how to find objects ______________________________.

Tash found out how to measure ______________________________.

The writer wanted to go camping ______________________________.

2 Circle the **simile** in *New Message*. Underline the **metaphor**.

Tip: *Could, would, should* and *might* are **auxiliary (helping) verbs**. They are often used with the **verb** *have*. Never use *of* in a **verb group**. *Of* is a **preposition**.

correct	*She might <u>have</u> gone home already.*
incorrect	*She might <u>of</u> gone home already.*

3 Choose a **verb group** from the box to complete each sentence.

might have
could have
should have
would have

I wish I ______________ gone camping.

I ______________ enjoyed camping.

My parents ______________ allowed me to go camping.

I ______________ been able to see Jupiter.

4 In the first paragraph of *New Message*, underline the **noun group** that labels the parents.

5 Underline the **noun groups** in each sentence.

My smart, witty, talented friend likes camping.

Tash's family is going camping.

I will look out my bedroom window.

I would have seen many constellations.

Many stars are visible away from the city lights.

6 Write an extended **noun group** to describe a member of your family. Use a dictionary for help.

7 Find and circle the **complex sentence** in *New Message* that includes the **conjunction** *if*. Underline the **independent clause** in the sentence.

Tip

Informal language, used between family members and friends, can include **slang** (e.g. *sick/sic for something good*) and **idiomatic expressions** (e.g. *beating around the bush meaning 'not getting to the point'*). **Idiom** means something that can't be worked out from the words used.

8 Write the **slang** word used in *New Message*. Then write what it means in *New Message*.

9 Copy the two **idiomatic expressions** in *New Message*. What do they mean?

10 Write two **slang** words or **idioms** used by your friends or family members. What do they mean?

11 Find and write six describing **adjectives** used in *New Message*.

12 Write four **verb groups** that use **modal verbs** in *New Message*.

13 What is your **opinion** of the writer of *New Message* and their complaint?

Try it yourself!

Write an **informal** text as a **response** to something positive or negative that has happened to you. Use **similes**, **metaphors** and **idioms** as well as interesting **noun groups**.

Unit 32

Commands, conjunctions, tongue-in-cheek humour

This imaginative text provides a set of **instructions**. It uses **tongue-in-cheek humour** to entertain. It has a series of **commands** that tells what to do in an imaginary situation.

WHAT TO DO IF ALIENS LAND IN YOUR NEIGHBOURHOOD

- STAY WELL CLEAR; DON'T GO NEAR.
- HIDE UNDER THE BED OR IN A TREE.
- TAKE POTS, PANS AND OTHER LOUD BANGING IMPLEMENTS TO SCARE OFF THE ALIENS.
- KEEP QUIET UNLESS THEY FIND YOU.
- IF THEY FIND YOU, BANG LOUDLY ON YOUR POTS AND PANS.
- IF BANGING FAILS TO SCARE THEM, HAVE WATER BOMBS OR A GARDEN HOSE NEARBY, BECAUSE THEY WON'T LIKE WATER.
- IF THEY APPROACH YOU, SCREAM UNTIL YOUR THROAT IS HOARSE.
- IF THEY ARE STILL COMING AT YOU, RUN AWAY VERY QUICKLY AND DON'T LOOK BACK.
- IF THEY GRAB YOU FROM BEHIND, BITE THEM.
- OR, DROP ON THE GROUND AND ROLL IN THE DIRT SO YOU WILL NOT TASTE GOOD IF THEY BITE YOU.
- REPORT TO YOUR LOCAL GOVERNMENT OFFICE.

Tip The instructions *What to Do if Aliens Land in Your Neighbourhood* are written in a way that seems serious but is actually poking fun. This is called **tongue-in-cheek**.

1 Read *What to Do if Aliens Land in Your Neighbourhood*. What aspects of the text make it obvious that it is **tongue-in-cheek**?

____

____

Tip Some **conjunctions** are used to show condition. Something has to occur in order for something else to occur.

At the beginning of the first **clause**: *If they grab you from behind, bite them.*

Placed between two **clauses**: *Bite them if they grab you from behind.*

2 The **conjunction** *if* is used repeatedly in *What to Do if Aliens Land in Your Neighbourhood*. Write two other **conjunctions** used in the instructions. Explain their function in the text.

__________ ______________________

__________ ______________________

3 List the **verbs** used in the **commands** in *What to Do If Aliens Land In Your Neighbourhood*.

____

____

____

Grammar Rules! Student Book 5 (ISBN 9780655092537) © Tanya Gibb

4 Instructions are often written as **commands**. Rewrite these **questions** as **commands**.

Why don't you try hiding in a cupboard?

____

Would you be able to keep quiet while you hide?

____

Can you make water balloons to scare them off?

____

Could you scream at the aliens when they approach you?

____

Would you like to taste an alien?

____

Tip

The suffix *–ing* added to a **verb** can show present or past tense, depending on the **auxiliary verb**.

I <u>am</u> hiding. *I <u>was</u> hiding.*

5 Imagine you are practising what to do in the event of an alien invasion. Complete each sentence in the **present tense**. Use an **auxiliary** and a **verb** with the suffix *–ing*.

<u>I am staying well clear and not going near</u>.

I ______________ under the bed.

I ______________ quiet unless they find me.

I ______________ pots and pans to scare them.

I ______________ loudly on my pots and pans.

I ______________ until my throat is hoarse.

I ______________ away very quickly and I ______________ back.

I ______________ them. They ______________ yucky.

I ______________ on the ground and I ______________ in the dirt.

I ______________ to my local government office.

Try it yourself!

Find a set of **instructions** for something in your home or school. Rewrite them in a **tongue-in-cheek** way. Or write what you would do if aliens landed in your neighbourhood. Use **commands** that begin with a **verb** or **verb group**.

Unit 33

First- and third-person narrator, character, plot

These texts show how stories can be narrated. Text 1 is in the **third person**. The author chooses what to tell readers about characters' thoughts and feelings. Text 2 is told in the **first person** by Otto as the narrator.

Escape From Mars

Text 1

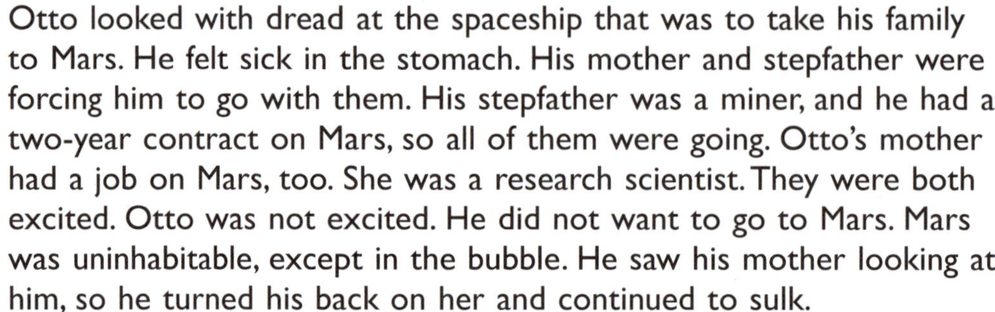

Otto looked with dread at the spaceship that was to take his family to Mars. He felt sick in the stomach. His mother and stepfather were forcing him to go with them. His stepfather was a miner, and he had a two-year contract on Mars, so all of them were going. Otto's mother had a job on Mars, too. She was a research scientist. They were both excited. Otto was not excited. He did not want to go to Mars. Mars was uninhabitable, except in the bubble. He saw his mother looking at him, so he turned his back on her and continued to sulk.

Jake saw Otto turn his back on them. He closed his eyes, regretting their decision to bring Otto along.

Text 2

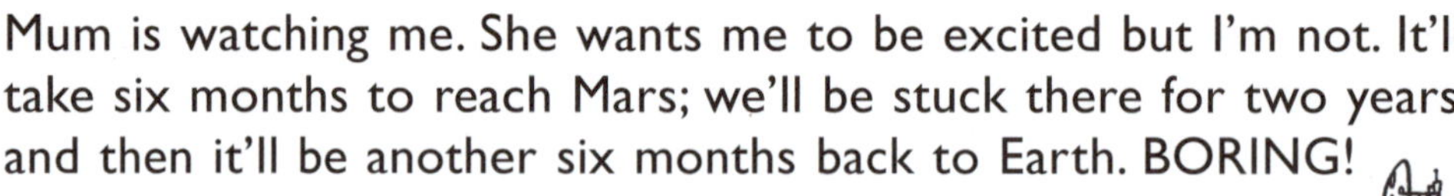

Mum is watching me. She wants me to be excited but I'm not. It'll take six months to reach Mars; we'll be stuck there for two years and then it'll be another six months back to Earth. BORING!

'I still don't see why I have to go,' I said.

Mum's lips went thin. She stared back at me, slowly shaking her head.

Tip In a **third-person** narrative, the author writes about characters as *he, she, they*.
In a **first-person** narrative, the narrator is a character in the narrative. First-person narratives use the pronouns *I, we, us*.

1 Read both texts in *Escape From Mars*. Whose **point of view** is shown in each text? How do you know the points of view?

Text 1 ______________________________

Text 2 ______________________________

2 Summarise what you know about the **characters** so far in *Escape From Mars*.

Otto ______________________________

Mum ______________________________

Jake ______________________________

3 What might Mum be thinking and feeling in Text 2? Write a **first-person** text from her point of view.

____

____

4 In *Escape From Mars*, what does, Mum's lips went thin, imply?

____

Grammar Rules! Student Book 5 (ISBN 9780655092537) © Tanya Gibb

5 What might the bubble in *Escape from Mars* be?

6 In *Escape From Mars*, why is 'BORING!' written in capital letters?

7 Write five **emotive** words used in Text 1.

Tip

Narratives require **conflict** or complications to keep readers interested. Conflict can involve problems between characters, between characters and nature, between characters and a society's rules, or characters can experience internal conflict as they deal with problems and meet challenges.

8 Based on *Escape From Mars* so far, what types of **conflict** does the plot include? Explain.

9 Write three predictions about what could happen in the **plot** of *Escape From Mars* based on the title.

10 If it's true that characters grow and change as the result of events in a plot, how might Otto grow as a person in *Escape From Mars*? What might he learn about himself and others?

11 What do you think of Otto's attitude and behaviour? Explain.

12 Does Otto seem like someone you'd like or dislike? Can you empathise with his point of view? Explain.

Try it yourself!

Write a **narrative**. Plan your plot to include **conflict** or problems for characters to resolve. Write in the **first** or **third person**. Make sure you tell readers what the main **character** is thinking and feeling during events in the **plot**. Help readers empathise with characters.

Unit 34

Reference, cohesion, connectives, nouns

This persuasive text is a **discussion**. It uses **connectives** to link and compare different **points of view** on a topic.

THE COST OF SPACE

The exploration of space is enormously costly to any country involved.

Many scientists believe the exploration of space is critically important and will benefit all humankind because of advances in technology, such as communications satellites, medical advances, water filtration systems and air purifiers. Some people even believe that Australia should get more involved than it has been, or it will miss an opportunity to be at the forefront of scientific research.

On the other hand, critics of the exploration of space argue that its benefits do not justify its costs and that the money could be better spent on things like hospitals and action on climate change. The average person would think that these things are far more important than sending a person to stand on the Moon or sending a camera to photograph red sand on Mars.

Nevertheless, most people are happy to support the exploration of space as long as money isn't squandered and they can see tangible advances in science as a result.

1 Read *The Cost of Space*. Summarise the two opposing **points of view** about space exploration.

____

____

2 Summarise the writer's conclusion in *The Cost of Space*.

____

The use of **nouns/noun groups** and **pronouns** for the same person, place, animal, thing or idea across a text makes a text **cohesive** and interesting.
Andy Thomas – He – This amazing NASA astronaut – An Adelaide boy – Andy

3 Circle the **nouns**, **noun groups** and **pronouns** that refer to the Space Shuttle *Discovery*.

The Space Shuttle *Discovery* has been on many space missions. It was first flown in 1984 and it was involved in a number of important voyages. This amazing spacecraft was one of three shuttles in NASA's space program. As well as *Discovery*, NASA sent the shuttles *Endeavour* and *Atlantis* on missions.

Grammar Rules! Student Book 5 (ISBN 9780655092537) © Tanya Gibb

Sometimes texts are presented as fact when they really portray the author's point of view. This can be subtle or obvious.

4 Do you think *The Cost of Space* portrays the author's **point of view**? If so, what do you think that point of view might be?

____

5 Do you think the ideas presented in the **discussion** *The Cost of Space* were balanced or biased? Explain your reasoning.

____

____

____

6 If you were an astronaut, what would be your **point of view** on *The Cost of Space?*

____

____

7 If you were a person in a developing country that did not have a space program, what might your **point of view** be?

____

____

8 Each sentence contains a **connective** that compares. Complete each sentence.

Remember the rule on page 38.

Space exploration is expensive. Nevertheless, ______________________________

____

Despite space exploration being so expensive, ______________________________

____

Whereas space exploration is very expensive, ______________________________

____

9 In *The Cost of Space* underline the **connectives** that compare.

10 Use each **connective** to compare in a sentence.

however	______________________________
yet	______________________________
although	______________________________

Have a spoken **discussion** with family members or class members about a topic that you know will raise different points of view. Record the discussion. Introduce alternative arguments without using 'I'. For example, *Some people believe that...; Other people agree that...; Most students realise that....* Use **connectives** to structure your writing.

Unit 35 Revision

1 Choose words from the box to complete each sentence.

would have might have could have should have

I wish I ________________ had a sleepover.

I ________________ helped you clean your room.

My sister ________________ allowed me to borrow her jacket.

I ________________ finished my essay on time but I left my book at school.

2 What does the underlined **idiomatic expression** mean?

'I'll do my homework later,' promised Zara.

'And <u>pigs will fly</u>!' responded Mum.

____

3 Write a **simile** to describe each setting.

a red sunset ____

hot sand at the beach ____

dark clouds in the sky ____

4 Rewrite each set of sentences as one **complex sentence**.

Rubbish has been left on the moon. It will be collected one day.

____

The word *galaxy* comes from the Greek word *galactos*. *Galactos* means 'the milky thing in the sky'.

____

____

In Western astronomy, the Milky Way is named after the Greek goddess Hera. Her milk sprayed across the sky.

____

____

The Milky Way Galaxy is a collection of stars, dust and gas. The Milky Way is over 13 billion years old.

____

____

Mars is rich in iron. Iron rusts and looks red. Mars is referred to as the red planet.

____

Grammar Rules! Student Book 5 (ISBN 9780655092537) © Tanya Gibb

5 Write a **paragraph** to describe a **character** for a story you might write. Use **pronouns** and interesting **noun groups** to refer to the character.

____

____

____

____

6 Rewrite each **sentence** in the **future tense**.

Isla launched her new drone.

____

Harlow recognised Venus through the telescope.

____

Praveena wrote a list of instructions.

____

7 Add to or change the end of each **noun** or **verb** to make a word for a person associated with it.

flora ____________________ spectate ____________________

photograph ____________________ law ____________________

bakery ____________________ architecture ____________________

library ____________________ celebrate ____________________

8 Write a paragraph that uses all the **connectives** in the box to show a time sequence.

eventually
then
after
next

____

____

____

____

____

9 Use the **connectives** in the box to show time sequence in this recount. If the **connective** begins a sentence, it needs a capital letter.

after	when	finally	at first	since	while	during	before	because

____________ dinner Dad received a phone call. ____________ he was on the phone, Mum told us a joke she heard at work that day. ____________ Dad returned to the table, we had to tell him Mum's joke. ____________ he didn't get it but ____________ he saw the funny side. ____________ everyone else had finished eating and ____________ Dad finished last, he had to do the dishes. ____________ the dishes were done, we all played board games ____________ we went to bed.

Glossary

Look at the page number in the circle to find more information about the rule or tip.

acronym............a word made up of the initial letters of other words (39)

adjective...........a word that tells more about a **noun**

adjectival clause (15) *adjectival phrase* (10) (59)
to classify (14) *comparative and superlative* (59)
to describe (10) *for possession* (15)
to quantify or tell number (14)

adverb................a word that adds meaning to a **verb**, **adjective** or another **adverb**; can tell time (when), place (where) or manner (how) (21)

modal adverbs (14) *adverb group* (21)

antonyms..........words with opposite meanings (17)

article.................(*a, an, the*) used in front of a **noun** or at the beginning of a **noun group** (10)

authoritative source.....a source of information that lends credibility to a claim (46)

clause.................a unit of meaning that includes a **verb** (8)

dependent clause (9) (11)
main (independent) clause (9) (11)

cohesion............how a text holds together using reference or **connectives** (23) (74)

comma...............a punctuation mark that separates:

a dependent clause from a main clause (23) (74)
items in a series (13)
prepositional phrases (13)
quoted speech (48)

command..........a sentence that tells someone to do something (70)

complex sentence.....includes an **independent clause** plus one or more **dependent clauses** (9)

compound sentence..a sentence consisting of two **independent clauses** (8)

conjunction........a word than joins **clauses** (12) (70)

coordinating (joins independent clauses in a compound sentence) (8)
subordinating (joins a dependent clause in a complex sentence) (12)

connective.........a word or word group that links ideas in a text (38)

determiners.......words that identify or point out (14)

emotive language.....used to evoke an emotional response from readers/listeners (24) (64)

exclamation.......an utterance spoken loudly or in surprise or anger (47)

first-person narrative....a story told by one of the characters using *I* or *we* (72)

formal/informal language....how language varies in formality according to the situation and audience (37) (51) (63) (69)

idiom...................an expression that is understood but means something different from the meaning of the words (69)

inclusive language ... language that is respectful and inclusive of diversity and gender 57

informal language ... see formal language

main idea ... the idea the writer or speaker wants you to believe or accept as true 14

metaphor ... figurative language where one thing is said to be another 51

narrative conflict ... tension in a plot that keeps readers/viewers interested 73

noun ... a naming word for people, places, animals, things and ideas 10
noun group 10 14 *singular and plural* 11 34

objective language ... language that is factual and unbiased 27

personal pronoun ... a word that refers to or replaces a **noun** 9

personification ... when human qualities are given to non-human things 14

possessive apostrophe ... a punctuation mark used to show possession 26

possessive pronoun ... a pronoun that shows possession 26

prefix ... letters or a word part added to the beginning of a word 17

prepositional phrase ... a group of words that consist of a **preposition** followed by a **noun** or **pronoun**; tells place (where), time (when) and manner (with whom, what or how) 18
can modify a noun (adjectival phrase) 10 59

pronoun reference ... the use of a pronoun to refer to the same **noun** across a text 74

question ... a sentence that asks for information or an opinion 40

quoted (direct) speech ... the actual speech someone said 33

reported (indirect) speech ... speech that is reported and not directly quoted 56

sentence ... a group of words that makes sense and includes at least one **verb** 8
complex sentence 9 *compound sentence* 8
simple sentence 8 *statement* 40

simile ... when something is compared to something else using *like* or *as* 51

subjective language ... shows a point of view, opinion or bias 27

suffix ... a letter/letters added to the end of words 35 49

synonym ... words that have similar meanings 44

tongue-in-cheek humour a kind of humour derived from pretending to be serious about something 70

verb ... a doing (action), being (relating), saying or thinking word 11
agreement with a noun (subject) 11 *auxiliary (helping)* 11 22
doing 11 *modal verbs* 16 *relating (being)* 11
saying 11 *tense* 22 28 71 *thinking* 11
verb group 11 16

voice ... the volume, pitch, pace, pause and tone of speech used for effect 45

word base ... the root or stem of a word to which affixes are added 52